SEEKING ENLIGHTENMENT

The Spiritual Journey of a Psychotherapist

SEEKING ENLIGHTENMENT

The Spiritual Journey of a Psychotherapist

CATHERINE H. MORRISON

TWO HARBORS PRESS | *Minneapolis*

Two Harbors Press
212 3rd Avenue North, Suite 290
Minneapolis, MN 55401
612.455.2293
www.TwoHarborsPress.com

ISBN - 978-1-935097-91-4
ISBN - 1-935097-91-1
LCCN - 2011941931

Printed in the United States of America

This book is dedicated with love and gratitude
to my teacher Sri Swami Dayananda Saraswati

CONTENTS

THE KING JAMES VERSION OF THE HOLY BIBLE

Genesis: c. 28: v. 10–17

10 And Jacob went out from Beersheba, and went toward Haran.

11 And he lighted upon a certain place, and tarried there all night, because the sun was set; and he took of the stones of that place, and put *them for* his pillows, and lay down in that place to sleep.

12 And he dreamed, and behold a ladder set up on earth, and the top of it reached to heaven: and behold the angels of God ascending and descending on it.

13 And, behold, the LORD stood above it, and said, I *am* the LORD God of Abraham thy father, and the God of Isaac: the land whereon thou liest, to thee will I give it, and to thy seed;

14 And thy seed shall be as the dust of the earth, and thou shalt spread abroad to the west, and to the east, and to the north, and to the south: and in thee and in thy seed shall all the families of the earth be blessed....

16 And, behold, I *am* with thee, and will keep thee in all *places* wither thou goest.... And Jacob awakened out of his sleep and said surely...[this place]...*is* none other but the house of God, and this *is* the gate of heaven.

INTRODUCTION

Piaget's Cognitive Stages as a Platform
for Emotional Development

Seeking Enlightenment is both a personal and a professional memoir. It is a true story. Every episode and every
character, though disguised for confidentiality, did exist or
actually happen. When I began this book, I did not know
Swami Dayananda. I was developing a logical system for
clarifying psychological stages from their beginning in
infancy to their culmination in Western mental health. I
called this end-point Autonomy. After I met the swami and
began learning about Eastern enlightenment, I spoke with
him about my project as, unlike most Indian gurus, he is
keenly interested in Western psychology and has educated
himself in the subject. He suggested that I extend the concept of Autonomy to include Eastern psychology, or, as he
called it: Ultimate mental health. This book is the result.

In it I use myself as a guide and, when appropriate,
as an example to illustrate my staging system. My theory
is an evolutionary one, beginning with a first set of six dysfunctional states starting with psychosis. Then it moves on
to a midlevel set of six "neurotic" states and ends with six
spiritual states that resolve in Enlightenment. (1)

Over the course of a long career, I worked in many

and varied settings. I was first a caseworker in a Department of Public Welfare; then I became a master's level social worker and practiced in a medical hospital. From there I worked in a psychiatric hospital, then in a child outpatient clinic, then in an adult outpatient clinic. During much of this time, I was raising a daughter as a single mother, carefully observing her development and introspective about my own reactions to life experiences, both in and out of my home. Also, throughout these years, I maintained a private practice.

I was trained in psychoanalytic theory, in Jungian psychology, in ego psychology, in developmental theory, and in other modalities as they developed. While none of these alone seemed an adequate treatment tool, taken together they served better to explain the human experience and to provide more effective therapy for the first two levels of development. However, not one of them, not even Jungian psychology, sufficiently explored or explained— and most never even mentioned—spiritual growth and development.

As a young therapist, this rather significant omission of spirituality did not concern me. I had been raised in literal Southern Protestantism, and I took my Christianity seriously until I fell in love with an Israeli at a Harvard summer program. He was the first Jew I had ever met, and because he did not "take Jesus Christ as his personal savior" *my* religion damned him to hell. This was ludicrous to me, and that realization served instantly to blow apart my tightly held but brittle brand of Christianity. From this moment on I lived for many years as a happy humanist, unconcerned with religion of any kind, applying myself instead to psychotherapy and the rest of my worldly life.

As I worked, I began to see two things. First, there was an order in the developmental process. Second, if halted, this ongoing sequence left a child or an adult emotionally stuck at the point of developmental delay. Thus, the problems in older children and adults mimic the essence of one or another task that had been bypassed and, therefore, structurally unresolved at the chronologically appropriate time. While physical and superficial emotional growth almost invariably took place around an unresolved "core" issue (and often obscured it), these bypassed developmental tasks remained inhibiting factors in individuals' lives and deprived them of deeper well-being and of a sense of satisfaction until or unless they were resolved by experience or in psychotherapy.

My work continually demonstrated that the normal developmental tasks of childhood paralleled, one for one, the residual or "leftover" pathology in adults, and thus maturation was a progressive and completely orderly system, not the chaos it had seemed when I began my therapeutic career. The realization of this order drew me increasingly to Jean Piaget, the Swiss psychologist who had classified cognitive development. He was by far the clearest and most definitive psychologist I knew. The elegant structural system that he had devised for the intellect provided a solid framework on which I could classify the emotional developmental sequence. Piaget had predicted that his cognitive system would allow for this if it were applied to emotions, and I saw that he was right.

His structure consists of three "plateaus," as he called them. Each plateau has six stages, the sixth stage doubling as the conclusion of its plateau and as the initiation of the succeeding one. This system yields sixteen stages altogether. I have used the word *plateau* because Piaget did, but it is misleading. It implies a horizontal plane, whereas development along a plateau is vertical. It moves upward, rung by rung. I think Piaget used "plateau" to emphasize that, on each of three levels, the material under construction is similar in kind, and in that sense each plateau *is* flat.

Piaget added one more element to his model of development. He said learning takes place in three *layers*. It begins at the first external intellectual layer, moves on to the second behavioral (or, I would say, emotional) layer, and then it reaches the third layer of core development, where structural change is internalized and solidified.

First-plateau children, from birth until eighteen months, see the world piecemeal, like a disassembled puzzle, and undertake the job of learning by sorting and fitting the pieces together. Here, the quintessential parts are their own bodies. Children move off the first plateau, having unified immediate space, pieced together toys and other objects within their small orbits, but most importantly, they have come to understand their bodies as wholes, distinct from things and other bodies. Piaget called this the plateau of "sensorimotor" intelligence. Here development is measured in behavioral change because infants are not yet able to think with pictures, symbols, or words, so they rely on action to express themselves. If sensorimotor development is thorough, young children celebrate their growth by stepping onto the second plateau as separate beings. If not, the older child or the immature adult remains psychologically dysfunctional with a first-plateau "defect" that he carries on into adult life.

On the first plateau, the unconscious mind performs the necessary psychological tasks for all of us. This process starts at birth, and I have described the critical tasks to be completed in Chapters 5 and 6.

There is an allegory in which six blind men, curious to know an elephant, had one brought before them, and each man felt the animal to discern its shape. One man felt the trunk; another, a leg; a third, the tail; a fourth, an ear; while a fifth and sixth felt a side and a tusk, respectively. I don't know if the blind men ever consolidated their findings to produce an elephant concept, but I do know that many of us "blind" human beings haven't managed to "whole" our parts. So if reincarnation exists, as the Buddhists say, it might give us additional opportunities to get ourselves together.

At eighteen months, second-plateau children devote themselves to the development of representational thought and the honing of concrete logic, which children employ between years seven to eleven. Piaget calls second-plateau thought "concrete" because it is tied to the literal ordering of mental images. The same holds true for emotional growth. Here children carry out mathematical operations and problem-solve, for example, by manipulating X number of apples or balls in their heads versus in their hands, as "concrete operations consist of nothing more than a direct organization of immediately given (mental) data." (2) Here the task is to understand and order self and things in representational thought. If successful, children move off this plateau knowing they have an inner life with thoughts and feelings of their own, just as other people have their own inner lives. Children who resolve second-plateau tasks reach what Western psychology calls maturity and what I call Autonomy. Unlike first-plateau work, we can consciously observe the psychological growth belonging to the second plateau if we wish to notice it. I have described these tasks in Chapter 7. Without successfully completing the second-plateau, a child enters adult life with a neurosis.

Finally, development brings us to the third plateau that Piaget called "formal operations" and that I designate "psycho-spiritual." I have described its tasks in Chapter 10. On this third plateau, Piaget and I interpret the work differently, although we'd probably agree that it is the most enthralling plateau of the three. Here Piaget studies solely abstract cognitive development at what I would call a "superficial" first or intellectual psychic level, while I study spirituality at the third or core level of the psyche.

All human beings have the same issues to resolve. Many people are not aware that they are problem-solving while the enigmatic work is taking place, but that is irrelevant. The important thing is that resolution happens. I became aware of my underlying process when I was in graduate school because I was studying psychology and trying to help myself and other people solve its sequential tasks. In this book, I use my own experiences (and those of my clients) as the "content" exhibiting these tasks. It doesn't matter that our content is always unique. What does matter is that the underlying structure we are developing is exactly the same. Though "wrapped" in different "dress" or "experience," the potential or latent psychic structure we may develop is uniform.

Continuing with the puzzle as metaphor, Piaget's third-plateau adolescents or young adults confront the task of ordering whole sets of puzzles and putting them in coherent categories by mental manipulation. This is his plateau of abstract thought or "formal operations". With abstraction, adolescents can arrange their puzzle sets in order of complexity or theme or size or any other sort of grouping they choose. Formal operations utilize abstract thought and the processes of "hypothetical and deductive reasoning."

A student of Piaget's once described formal operations as a scaffold that would allow the acrobat/thinker/subject to move with freedom from any one place on the structure to any other place he might fancy, and to return again if he so chose. The scaffold allowed that he would never get stuck but was always free to move at will. The same holds true for the "emotional scaffold" that I was building. With the structure complete, freedom to articulate unlimited nuances of feeling would be the norm.

Piaget explained his third plateau as normal adolescent cognition, seeming to have little or nothing to do with core development. While a child could get stuck at any stage along the developmental continuum, as one might expect, the further he progressed, the less severe and disabling the consequences of an impasse in core development became. Furthermore, autonomous people (at Stage

XI in my staging system) are psychologically mature and can live sane and happy lives even without using their third-plateau capacity for abstraction very much or very often. As such, third-plateau growth seemed less critical and less profound than first- and second-plateau development, which have already left their successful graduate with a mature ego and a solid character structure. What more does anyone need? As a therapist, I could not recall, nor could I even imagine, someone coming to therapy complaining of a third-plateau problem. Such a question would more likely be put to a college professor or perhaps a religious mentor. So did core-developmental work become inconsequential here as it seemed to do?

I lived with this unanswered question of third-plateau development for quite a long while, feeling relatively contented with my own growth, enjoying working with my clients and seeing them grow on the first two plateaus which Piaget's cognitive work had helped me develop for emotions. As some of my clients reached maturity, they were able to feel a new clarity about life's issues. They solved problems more easily and accepted disappointments more gracefully. Their lives were relatively happy, and they were satisfied that they had completed their therapy. I, too, was pleased with their progress. Autonomy was a welcome relief for all of us, and so I was surprised to become aware of an increasing feeling of ennui in myself.

I began to wonder if this sense of something missing could be related to that third level of development, about which I knew so little. Unable to find an answer, I absorbed myself in writing a book for therapists, clients, and other people who might simply be interested in the therapeutic process. (In my personal experience, this group seemed surprisingly large, with several people engaging me in small "therapy" discussions at most social events I attended.) I had long collected notes for such a project, and I had been mentally placing clients and others whom I knew well enough on my Piagetian emotional continuum for years. My working title was *Jacob's Ladder*.

However, feeling discontented, I became increasingly interested in Jacob and the place of his dream, which he called the "gate of heaven." I was also increasingly curious about those angelic beings ascending and descending upon a ladder and in God standing above telling Jacob that his seed would multiply and be "as the dust of the earth," spreading in all directions and blessing all people. Intensely inquisitive about what all of this meant and, after hearing the Dalai Lama read from the sacred Tibetan religious texts (see Chapter 8), knowing that there *had* to be a third spiritual plane on which to place people like him, I felt sure that such beings would someday populate my empty third plateau.

Since those early days at Harvard, and even before I met the Dalai Lama, my interest in some sort of god had been resuscitated. It no longer made sense to me that this complex world had come into being without an intelligent designer, but I was sure that such a creator would bear no resemblance to the false god I had discarded so many years ago. This force or source would be someone or something entirely new to me, and having spent so much time walled off behind Autonomy, I was eager to explore the new realm. So, while I wrote *Jacob's Ladder* and continued to work as a therapist, I began meditating and reading Eastern philosophy.

Then, when I met Swami Dayananda, and he taught the deep growth work possible on the third plateau, I understood that if one wished to proceed with core spiritual evolution, he could do so. And, hopefully, if he did wish to proceed, his decision would coincide with that of a guru and with God's larger purpose for his life.

However, if I am to do justice to the developmental story and its critical scaffolding, I must begin at the beginning of the one I know best--my own.

Catherine Morrison
March 2011

NOTE

Psychology has its own jargon, which may be shorthand for psychologists but is opaque to others. Mostly, I have avoided it, but I use a few terms in this book that I will define here so that the reader knows my intended meaning:

(1) A *dyad* is a couple so closely bound that they operate as a unit. A mother and her newborn baby form a dyad, whereas the baby and its sitter are only a pair. If a couple of adults form a dyad, they are symbiotically interconnected and poorly defined as individuals.

(2) The verb *project* means to perceive one's own thoughts as external to oneself. They can be experienced as arising from an unseen, outside source—as in an auditory hallucination—but more commonly they are imagined as the thoughts of other people. In either case they are subjective phenomenon mistakenly seen as objective reality.

(3) One who projects *externalizes* his thoughts.

(4) By contrast, *internalization* is (usually) a healthy process whereby external experience is taken in and digested, becoming part of one's own evolving psyche.

(5) Last, confounded by the problem of gender in third-person-singular English pronouns, I have used "he" alone instead of "he and/or she" together, which seems awkward.

CLARIFICATION

Various spiritual teachers use different English terms to designate their meaning of *atman* or *Brahman*. In Vedic literature, *Brahman* means the absolute, the supreme being, the creator. The first person in the Hindu trinity, *Brahman* is followed by *Vishnu* and *Shiva*. *Atman* refers to *Brahman* in the individual person. It is not exactly equivalent to Christianity's soul, but the two are close in meaning. Swami Dayananda often uses "consciousness" or "unity consciousness" to refer to *Brahman* or Ultimate Mental Health. The Hindu Upanisads use "consciousness" to mean the Ultimate State. Swami Tattvavidananda uses *Isvara* or "awareness." Evelyn Underhill uses "The Unitive Life." Nisargadatta Maharaj uses the term awareness to mean realization and consciousness to mean simply holding a thing in mind.

In describing the psychological development of the observational ego in Part II, I have used the terms "witness consciousness," "consciousness," and "awareness." I think my intended meaning will be clear from the context, and in Part III, we will see a distinction between the Western psychological definition of these terms and the Eastern spiritual meaning they hold. In Western psychology, the terms consciousness, awareness, and witness consciousness are restricted to use as "pseudo-seers," objects to the "Self;" whereas, in spiritual parlance, these terms refer to the Source, "The-One-Without-A-Second," unseen, but all-seeing.

ACKNOWLEDGMENTS

My thanks to the many people who have helped me with
this book, especially Sharon Cliff, Martha Dorothy, and
Alakananda Bhujle from Arsha Vidya Gurukulam. Sharon
read the manuscript, in one of its early drafts for Swami
Dayananda, and Martha and Alakananda gave me valuable
help, including assistance with some Sanskrit words and their
meanings. David Elliott, PhD, and Susan Kesling, LICSW,
read the manuscript for theoretical clarity and made invaluable corrections and suggestions. My thanks and gratitude
to Swamini Srividyananda and Sri Shivcharan Gupta for
the cover photograph of the temple's lotus doors and for the
dedication picture of Swami Dayananda. My thanks also to
Vimila Sadasivam for her help in supplying me with several
important facts and with some Sanskrit terms I needed. My
unbounded gratitude to Ananthanarayanan Gopalam for the
technical help given me with the final form of the fold-out
chart. I also thank Two Harbors Press for their patience in
handling my many rounds of revisions.

SOME NOTES ON THE EXPOSURE AND
TESTING OF THIS THEORY

Joan Borysenko, PhD; Ilan Kutz, MD; and I had a chance to see my theory (at this point the first and second plateaus only) work as a diagnostic tool when assessing the status and progress of clients in Herbert Benson's Mind/Body Clinic in the early '80s. Our positive results in pairing meditation with psychotherapy were published as the lead article by I. Kutz, J. Borysenko, and H. Benson in the prestigious *American Journal of Psychiatry*, Vol. 142 (1), P. 1–8. These results were also published in 1985 as a paper titled *Meditation as an Adjunct to Psychotherapy* by I. Kutz, J. Leserman, C. Dorrington, C. Morrison, J. Borosenko, and H. Benson in *Psychotherapy and Psychosomatics*, Vol. 43, P. 209–218.

In the 1980s and since, I have taught my theory to social-work students at the Beth Israel and to social workers, psychologists, and psychiatrists at the Boston Institute for Psychotherapy. More recently, David Elliott, PhD, teaches it and other theories to students overseas through the International School for Psychotherapy, Counseling and Group Leadership.

EPIGRAPH

As the mountainous depths
of the ocean
are unmoved when waters
rush into it,
so the man unmoved
when desires enter him
attains a peace that eludes
the man of many desires.
When he renounces all desires
and acts without craving,
possessiveness,
or individuality, he finds peace.
This is the peace of the infinite spirit;
achieving it, one is freed from delusion;
abiding in it even at the time of death,
one finds the pure calm of infinity.

—The Bhagavad Gita II: 69–72

PART I:

GLIMPSING MY IGNORANCE

CHAPTER 1:

Beginning

I am just pulling up the emergency brake in the black Chevrolet with *Gaston County Department of Public Welfare* embossed on both doors, when Netti Erps pokes her head through the open window on the passenger's side.

"Bet you don't know what happened here last night."

"No, I don't," I reply, certain from her demeanor that I don't want to know either.

"Etta Mae got drunk as a skunk, and so did Billy Ray. He drew nasty pictures all over her with lipstick and locked her outside the house in nothin' but her chiff. And all three children, too. They was out there most of the night howling and screechin'. They wouldn't stop, and Billy wouldn't open the door. He just lay up there laughin' out loud. I told 'em I'd tell the welfare lady first chance I git, and here you is!" She smiles triumphantly, as though she's conjured me up out of quantum potential all by herself.

I know, as the official representative of the department, I'm expected to have a huge reaction, as though that would change anything, but I'm not clear what Nettie needs to hear. Is her complaint against the noise, the drinking, Billy Ray, her erstwhile best friend Etta, the treatment of the children, the welfare system in general, or some combination of these. Sensing my dilemma, she supplies a clue, "It ain't *right*, gettin' the check and actin' like *that*." So her problem does include some of all the above.

"I'll speak to Etta Mae and Billy Ray," I say, and I do. By the time I reach her house, Etta has her clothes on, but there is a crude phallic-shaped object protruding onto her left forearm from under her blue and pink floral-print sleeve like a faded pink tattoo. It looks as though she has tried to wipe it away, probably when she heard my car, but there it sits like the blood on Bluebeard's key. Over a cup of tea, we talk about Netti's complaint. Etta says that Netti's jealous because she's sweet on Billy herself.

"The Lord knows why, since he's a shiftless bum who never done a lick of work in his life! He bought hisself some white lightnin' and barged in here. I couldn't git shed of him. But I tried. So he shut me out, and the children, too!" She waves her unadorned arm at her children as though to direct my attention to the innocent and away from herself. I think of mother quail performing the opposite maneuver, drawing hunters' attention to themselves and away from their nestlings.

The children in question always cluster around me, staring. Their noses run with varying hues of yellow-green mucus. They are curious about this familiar stranger in their midst. I am different. I have a peculiar power in their world. Though they range in age from fourteen months to three years, they share the same expression. It defies description, at once anxious, depressed, listless, hopeless, and watchful. They seem to be saying, "Things never improve around here, but they can fall apart any minute; maybe right now, and you may be the one to make it happen." I always try to avoid looking at this expression. I keep my gaze pitched carefully over their heads. While they stare at me, I stare at their mother. But it's no use. I see the same expression there, too, just behind those falsely animated eyes, so I study the cracks in my teacup.

Etta and I have talked before about her going to work for the florist down the street as soon as her youngest is a little older. She once confided in me that she loved bright colors and pretty fragrances, though you'd never know it from sitting in her drab, faintly urine-scented shack. On some occasions, her false animation wanes, and the closed and hopeless expression she shares with her children falls away for a moment. Then I can see a real person. Today, that real Etta is not at home.

I can feel the news coming before it reaches her lips: "I think I'm pregnant. And it *ain't* Billy's!" A tall tale follows, about waiting at the bus stop and a man in the shadows trying to rape her while she struggles against him. Finally some Good Samaritans happen by and rescue her, chasing after the shadow man, who gets away, of course, since he was never there to begin with. As she blatantly lies, I try to read her attitude. Why? Not just why make yourself ridiculous by telling such stories as though you think anyone will believe them, but...*why?* Why live like this? It makes no sense, and sometimes she knows it. Defiance? Helplessness? Resignation? Does she think her life can never change? Does she want it to change?

We talk about the difficulty of her having and caring for a fourth child and about postponing the flower-arranging so indefinitely. But, of course, she wants to keep the baby anyway. Maybe her mother will move back from Florida this winter when jobs for fruit-pickers end. "Mama loves kids. She could help me with these babies." Etta lets her mask slip momentarily and shows a vague wistfulness as she speaks of her mother. Could her longing for mothering motivate this endless childbearing?

I ask if she misses her mother. She smiles an assent with which her eyes agree. "Do you think she might come back to help you one day if you get into deep enough trouble?" I ask. She smiles again, but this time it is the false expression. As quickly as she came, the real Etta disappears again behind that awful mask. The answer is no. She really doesn't think so, and neither do I. So she's living out the fantasy, that somehow she might *get* the thing she wants by *becoming* that thing. We can both see it isn't working. But she doesn't want to face that, and I can't take any more of it just now either, so I back off, all the while thinking, *My God, Etta's children are doomed to repeat their mother's fate. Even if there is a way out for them, I don't know what it might be.*

"Shall I tell Billy Ray he'd better be careful how he treats you? Your neighbors might call the police, and his making a fuss like last night around you and the children could get your check in trouble." Etta likes this idea and says now is a good time, because Billy is up at the corner gas station, and he'll have time to cool off before he gets back. But Etta tells me I shouldn't tell him she knew I was going to tell him. I should just say that Nettie told on him and that I was bucking mad. I said I would tell him the truth because it never helped to lie, and what he needed to understand *was* the truth.

We update the figures on Etta's Aid to Dependent Children budget. I walk to the corner to deliver my message to Billy and try not to think about my successors in the years to come visiting three more homes, and now a fourth, where they will encounter the same situation I am just leaving. This lifestyle of dissatisfaction and stagnation is destined to be handed down from mother to child as surely as Etta's surname was bequeathed to her by her own mother. Clearly Etta and her children need the meager subsistence funding they receive from the Welfare Department, but just as clearly they need something else more. They need that spark of fulfillment and hope, briefly glimpsed in Etta when she speaks of becoming a florist. They need this hope nurtured until, eventually, it might blaze up into flame and burn away the debris of rage and depression under which they lie suffocating, generation after generation. I am neither mandated nor equipped to deliver this service.

I climb back into my car and wave good-bye to Nettie, who is still watching me from across the street. The welfare lady—an ironic title, indeed—has done her job. Nettie can now release me back into the void from which I came. And she does.

I hate feeling helpless. I always have. So how could I have gotten myself into this impossible situation? It's my father's blindness that has brought me here, and I am still astonished to find myself in this bizarre job instead of in graduate school at Columbia University. Initially ignorant of the significance of seeing deeply, I do my job because it is my job and only gradually realize, and even more gradually admit, the effect this learning about others has on the deeper levels of my own psyche. It is after working many months that I begin to see myself transfixed by my routine encounters with people. Eventually they will transform me, but I deny their impact for years, even though I am unable to leave the field of interactive psychology.

When I first fail to leave, I give myself excuses. Then I settle in, telling myself that I can dignify social work as a developmental study of human psychology, a serious and worthwhile pursuit. Finally, I come to understand each of my interactions with another person, recorded here or not, as one tiny step in my own evolution. In clusters, these encounters comprise one rung on a very profound and very personal Jacob's ladder—one that confronts *every* human being, whether or not he chooses to accept the challenge. Aligning one's self to comprehend another person's alignment with increasing clarity forces one to observe essential psychic structure. And *knowledge* is power in the form of persisent *pressure* to change, to grow.

My life, like that of other human beings, is—as the Buddha rightly said—a cycle of pains and pleasures. For me, an early source of distress is my father's thirteen eye surgeries for retina detachment. Almost exactly at the time I graduate from college, he suffers a final unsuccessful surgery on a final detachment in his second eye, leaving him completely blind. My mother comes alone to my graduation. She is grief-stricken and, even though this outcome has been expected, when it finally happens I am stunned.

My mother tells me the news as I meet her after the ceremony, still in my cap and gown. She says, "You are the person to whom your father will listen most, and I need you at home now to help me with his rehabilitation." Reluctantly I agree to cancel my graduate school plans in New York, and instead I return to Gastonia, North Carolina. Since I can't type, the only job I can find is at the local welfare office as an untrained social worker distributing Aid to Dependent Children and other federal assistance programs to people who qualify.

I begin this job thinking I know what there is to know about Gastonia and its people. After all, I was born here and attended public school until I was sixteen. I was not particularly sheltered, and I was an active and adventurous child, but I will soon discover that my encounters with my hometown were limited indeed. While Gastonia has not changed much, I am going to change plenty and on many levels simultaneously, by seeing it through the eyes of a welfare worker. A different sort of "bell" has rung, and "classes" have begun for me.

Much to my surprise, for the most part I enjoy my welfare job, and it offers resources for helping my father previously unknown to me. Geraldine Hill is one of my colleagues. She is in charge of services to the blind under the larger category of Aid to the Permanently and Totally Disabled. Legally blind herself, she gets around independently using a cane. She is a kind woman who gives the impression of such great vulnerability and bravery, that no one could possibly take advantage of her. Instead, people move aside to let her pass. They help her across streets and drive her home when she has packages. She looks out through thick glasses, which so magnify her eyes that they fill the frames to the rim. I am curious but never ask how the world looks to her from the other side of those giant, slightly tremulous pupils.

I tell Geraldine about my father, and she tells me about the talking-book service from the Library of Congress and about Braille tutorials. She issues a special record player to my father so he can listen to *Newsweek*, *The Reader's Digest*, or novels—mailed back and forth from Washington to our front door in thick black boxes buckled with broad fabric straps. Geraldine gives me the government's Braille instruction books, and I order Braille playing cards since my father loves bridge and poker. He suffers through my lessons and learns to read but never enjoys Braille books or cards. However, as soon as he hears the postman at the door, he heads downstairs to pick up a new talking book. He listens to these by the hour.

The Gaston County Department of Public Welfare is housed in a former private residence. It is a rambling building, its wallpaper faded sepia and tarnished with water marks. The front parlor, outfitted with four rows of twelve folding chairs, serves as our waiting room. Clients sit in this cheerless place waiting for intake interviews or to discuss various matters with their caseworkers. From the wall opposite their chairs, a fireplace, no longer used even in cold weather, yawns vacantly as the seated figures wait. A large oak receptionist's desk faces the waiting area and the front door. It commands the room. This is Louise Morgan's post. Though she is called receptionist, Louise is so much more. It is she who keeps the office running. Effiency itself, she is loved and relied on by all of us, to answer the phones, take the messages, and get information to the right person promptly. She seems to know, instinctively, how to handle crises. When one of my Permanently and Totally Disabled clients has a grand mal seizure, she is instantly, almost miraculously, by his side, pencil in hand, ready to break his fall and depress his tongue so he won't swallow it if he loses consciousness. I pray Mr. Duncan won't repeat this performance when I am alone with him on a home visit.

To the left of Louise's desk, occupying the last third of the waiting room, is a closed-in porch, a sort of sun parlor, with glass-paneled French doors. It holds another desk and two folding chairs. It is the intake room. Caseworkers rotate this unpopular duty. Whoever is "on" occupies the sun parlor. Mr. Adams, our superintendent, is the only person with a private office. The rest of us are crowded into four rooms with two desks placed back to back and a third positioned with it's back to the sides of the others. This inelegant arrangement conserves space. When one of us needs the office for a client interview, the others take their dictation machines and folders of paperwork to the former kitchen, now a general secretarial room. If a client comes in while we are so displaced, we see him wherever we can find a vacant corner.

This is why I see Mr. Hamilton on the screened-in back porch one hot and sticky August afternoon. The air is heavy with moisture. I sigh frequently, conscious of forcing oxygen into my lungs. There is no such thing as air-conditioning at this office. It is especially striking when Mr. Hamilton, with every reason to be furious, *apologizes* as he tells me that his check is two weeks late.

He adds, "I don't mean to be uppity, but I can't ask for no more credit at the store." *Uppity?* I thought that word went out with carpet baggers. But apparently not. He means it.

Mr. Hamilton is a handsome black man with a large, powerful frame. His hair is cut short. It covers his head with tight grey curls. He is almost seventy years old and lives with his wife on the side of Crowder's Mountain near where our family housekeeper, Cora Gullick, was born and raised. The Hamiltons are farmers like Cora's people were. They still farm their land, though now on a small scale. They can their vegetables, milk their cow, gather eggs from their hens, and count on Old Age Assistance to pay for whatever they can't produce and for various services, which increase in cost year by year more quickly than public assistance rises to meet them. More and more, to avoid debt, the Hamiltons do without. Since he owns no car, he has traveled to the office that morning on foot and by bus. Now he stands in front of me, his eyes lowered, gazing at the floor just in front of my guilty feet. In one hand, this majestic man holds his hat. In the other, he holds a soggy handkerchief, which was probably crisp and white this morning. Now limp and grey, he uses it to blot his face and neck. The perspiration not absorbed by the already saturated cloth drips from his chin onto the bib of his roomy denim overalls.

I explain that I have made a clerical error and that some of my paperwork has just been returned from the state office that morning.

"I am very sorry. I am new, you see. I'm just making the necessary corrections now." In the meantime, I suggest that I could get some general assistance to tide him over. Maybe I can explain to the owner of the store where he trades.

Why on earth is a man like this using a word like "uppity" and apologizing for my mistake? I wonder. My body temperature rises even higher as the realization hits home. I can feel a deep scarlet flush ascend from the pit of my stomach and spread out over my face and neck like red dye. My father's fourth-cousin was Nathan Bedford Forrest, a Civil War general and first grand wizard of the Ku Klux Klan. The sins of our forefathers have been egregious, and now I understand they are not yet as dead and buried as I would wish. It is difficult to have a conversation with this man as one human being to another. He can't seem to let me. Brutality, hatred, greed, fear, guilt, shame—all the negative emotions I can think of seem to stand between us.

In that moment I realize there is also a gulf between Cora and myself. I have known Cora since I was a child. She is the black person I know and love best in the world. She calls me "her girl," and my mother complains that I "dog Cora's steps" so closely that she can't get her work done. Even though we once traveled to New York by bus together so she could visit her sister and I could visit a friend from school, I haven't seen until now how much fear instead of friendship played in that plan. Cora was *afraid* to travel alone because she was a black woman in a white world. She packed that shoebox full of her delicious fried chicken, deviled eggs, and pound cake, not just for our enjoyment, but so that she wouldn't have to rely on the kindness of strangers. I have not understood deeply enough, even about Cora. And just now, our parallel universes seem split by a rift so wide they might never meet, like Mr. Hamilton's eyes and mine as we stand together on this tiny, screened porch encased in different worlds.

"I'm really sorry, Mr. Hamilton," I repeat. "It's my mistake. Mrs. Hamilton has told me how important it is to you that your bills be paid ahead of time." Something about my distress seems to soften him. He lifts his gaze from the floor and allows our eyes to meet. He is a kind and gentle man who emanates integrity.

As high as the walls might be between Cora and Mr. Hamilton and myself, they seem minor compared to those between me and many other clients, like Jude Starker. The Welfare Department divides Gaston County into pie-shaped wedges. Each worker is responsible for one slice. Each slice includes a section of densely populated city at its central tip and widens to the less dense periphery of suburban outskirts where I live and on toward the crust-edge of sparsely populated rural farmland, where the Hamiltons live and where Cora grew up. Concentrated at the sharp angles are the city dwellers. In these central tips of dense city are the "slums," such as slums are in the rural South. Jude Starker lives in my section.

No one in the office except me likes working in this area. Perhaps *like* is too strong a word, but my view of the people in this community is quite different from that of most of my colleagues. No question this population is tough, but it is refreshing, too, in its own way. Jude is an especially rough customer. Face disfigured with scar tissue from a knife fight, she has an ugly scowl permanently affixed to the left side of her mouth, pulling its corner down toward her chin. On that same side, her eye is half closed by another scar running from the bridge of her nose, through her eyebrow, and into her scalp. Rather than try to soften the expression etched on one side of her face, Jude exaggerates it by willfully squinting and scowling on the right side.

You have to work hard to find Jude. She moves a lot, and also she is rarely at home. When I find her house and her at home, I always find her entourage of roustabout boyfriends, who are probably dope-peddlers, booze-runners, bookmakers, and Lord knows what else. On top of this, Jude makes me work hard and sweat plenty to extract the information I need to renew her paltry grant. She gets her money's worth out of the state, and out of my hide as well.

While Jude is always difficult and intimidating, I think I understand where she is coming from, and I respect her. She takes nothing lying down. She fights back on principle. She is one woman whose mouth never contorts into shapes framing words like "uppity." She knows her rights, not her place, and she emphasizes that fine distinction with every breath she draws. I had to admire that. As exaggerated as it is, she makes a valid point. She knows she has me, and all of us, by the short hairs. She insults me by her very attitude. She angers me. She intimidates me and sorely tries my patience. However, she never plays the victim or even the needy role. It is Jude's redeeming feature.

Earlier in the morning on the occasion of my fifth, and finally successful, attempt to locate Jude, I narrowly escape being mauled by a new client's dog with the apt name of "Buster." It is common for every house to have its watchdog, especially in the rural areas, but the viciousness of this beast is unusual. Jude doesn't have a dog. She doesn't need one. When I find her at home that afternoon, there is something more active than usual going on in her front room. Several men sit at a table with Jude, laughing and talking. Jude comes out on her porch as I approach. Through the screen door and the smoky haze behind her, I recognize two of the men. One is her sometimes boyfriend Jimmy, and the other is his locally infamous brother Jamie. Jamie is said to be a bootlegger. Other men drive into Jude's yard as regularly as bees to nectar. They move up and down the porch steps on one side while Jude and I stand on the other. Some of these men are familiar to me as regular visitors to Jude's house.

Jude proffers no explanation. She never hands me tall-tale cover stories. In fact she blatantly lies when the truth would serve her better and is also plainly visible to both of us. It is a game with her. Instead of inviting me inside, as is customary, Jude plants herself on the front porch at the top of the steps, smoking, as though to bar my entrance.

I stand in the yard beside the steps, eye level with her, one foot on the bottom step, trying to balance my papers on my knee. Her two children swing on the screen door just inside, looking out at us. I try awkwardly to break the ice, which never thaws with Jude. I pause between sentences, anyway, trying for a response.

"Well, how have you been? I've had a hard time finding you. I figured you must have moved. I sent you a letter asking you to come by the office or to notify me of your new address. Your checks would have stopped if I hadn't been able to review your grant with you today. Did you know that?"

"You found me," she answers in a lifeless tone.

"OK. Let's go over your grant."

"Nothing's changed, but the rent went up," she says, in that same tone.

"Well, who's living here with you now?" I have to ask this *ridiculous* question, because anyone living with her must share expenses, and her answer has to be in my record. She looks at me as though I am an even bigger fool than she'd ever and always thought. I truly feel like one. "Me and Clifford and James." She nods toward the two children who are swinging on the screen door and now close it with a loud bang and disappear inside. It is as though they have heard their names and don't want to get involved. They are Jude's sons, for sure.

"So you have no income now except your welfare check?"

"You got *that* right. Same as before." Pointedly, "Just like I *said* before."

This so-called conversation goes on for ten painful minutes with me, as always, feeling more and more idiotic, but I get the data I need for an official update of Jude's file.

"I guess that's it for the next six months," I say. "I'll see you again around Christmas. And you have to let us know if you move."

Jude spits into the yard, not exactly at me but clearly in my direction. Wrong choice of words. You can't say "have to" to Jude for any reason. She gives the impression she's killed for less, and I wouldn't bet against it.

Impulsively and a little recklessly, under the circumstances, I say, "What *are* they selling in there? Chances for heaven? Or just angel dust?" I am gratified to see an ever-so-slight smile-like motion flicker in the right-hand corner of Jude's mouth.

She straightens it instantly. In a mocking sing-song tone, pausing for sarcastic emphasis on every word, she says, "Jimmy makes book. And Jamie makes booze." The implication is, "If that's true, honky, you'll have to prove it first, and then just *try* to do something about it." I had never doubted this taunt, but I hadn't the least interest in proving it one way or the other. All I knew for sure was that Jimmie and Jamie were both inside Jude's house, as usual. I reckoned that Jude and her children usually lived with these two 'money-minting' brothers, but I wouldn't be the one to take it to court, and I couldn't imagine the imbecile who might. Not even my straight-laced supervisor would be so fool-hearty, and I would *also* place a bet on that.

"Jude," I say, "you are without a doubt the hardest woman I ever tried to give money to." This time, she can't help herself, and she smiles an especially crooked smile. I have made her day, and, actually, she has made mine, too. In two full years of sporadic contact, this is the closest I come to bridging a fragment of the gulf between us.

It does not take long to understand that the welfare system is like throwing sandbags at New Orleans levees with a category 5 hurricane bearing down. It gets very old, very fast. Material goods are all but useless in such emotional chaos. As a welfare worker, I feel impotent and empty with my clients. It is increasingly clear that I need to know a lot more than I do now if I ever hope to stand my ground, never mind make progress, with the clients I serve. Again, I vow to get out of here and go to graduate school in history or English. But certainly, if I ever work with people again, I will first get a very solid psychological education.

As if to underscore this resolution, about eighteen months into the so-called "rehabilitation" of my father, when I come home from work one afternoon, my mother meets me on the front steps, white with tension. She tells me that my father tried to kill himself today. Beginning to cry, she sits on the stair and between sobs, she tells me that he took all the sleeping pills he could find, thinking it was an overdose. Mother found him in bed, asleep, when she returned from school. She couldn't rouse him, and was immediately alarmed, so she called our family doctor, who interrupted his own schedule to attend this emergency. "He administered a shot of adrenalin," my mother continues, "and stayed with us, checking Emmett's pulse, and blood pressure until he was sure he was out of danger." She was crying now from relief as she repeated that Dr. Grey had assured her his patient was OK, now, and should wake up soon.

In the hours that follow, while the family clusters around my father's bed, I learn that earlier that morning he has placed his two life-insurance policies carefully on the living-room desk. The clauses that designate the money will be paid even in the event of suicide have been circled in red. Obviously he has done this years ago when he could still see, against the day, this day, when his sight would fail and he would no longer care to remain among us disabled. My mother tells us that this morning she left for school at 7:00 as usual. She had noticed nothing remarkable about my father or his attitude. She had returned home at 4:00 to find him, as though dead, asleep in this bed. She could barely feel a pulse, was very frightened and called the doctor immediately.

Five of us now stand around my father's bed awaiting his awakening—my brother, Emmett Jr.; his young wife, Rankin; their six-month-old son, Sid; my mother; and myself. My sister is away at college. Emmett Jr. and his family live in their own apartment in Gastonia, and he works as a manager in a local textile mill. None of us, including me, whose special job it is to tend his mental health, have realized my father is actively suicidal.

We talk about what to do. My mother can't stop working for financial reasons, especially since my father's eye problems have greatly curtailed his earning years. Emmett and Rankin say they will move in with us, so that he will not be at home alone during the weekdays while my mother teaches. Dad can live downstairs, in the guest bedroom with its own bath, where he will be at the center of family activity. Emmett and Rankin will occupy Emmett's old bedroom with the comfortable double bed. Young Sid and I will share the remaining room, next to his grandmother, across the hall from his parents and connected to their room by a second bathroom that the rest of us will share.

I look down at my new roommate. He is poised at my feet, looking up at me intently. Sid is not yet walking or talking, but he is bright, strong, and energetic. He cruises around on all fours at high speeds and with amazing agility. "Enthusiastic" is the word for Sid. He is the embodiment of joie de vivre in everything he does. It is part of his great charm. I have read about laughing eyes, but I'd never seen a pair before, not eyes that are always smiling like his.

The atmosphere in the room is anything but laughable just now. However, when our eyes meet, Sid and I laugh out loud. What a relief from this heavy ordeal that is. Glad of the promise of some action, he slaps the floor with his hands, spins around, and dashes off to get a game of chase going. I am delighted to accept the invitation, and in that moment we bond solidly and begin to play. Always a great playmate, he quickly lightens up the whole place, and by the time my father opens his poor sightless eyes, we are solidly prepared for his return to us and for supporting his recovery.

It is not long before we know he will never try to kill himself again. He makes it clear that he is deeply touched by our love for him and by our working together on his behalf. He will endure whatever he must to spare us a repetition of this ordeal. Though he quickly assures us of his safety, it is many months before he recovers his formerly cheerful personality. Eventually, he is himself again. He lives another twenty-eight years and plays a significant role in my daughter's childhood and in the lives of his other grandchildren. I think these years with his grandchildren may have been the happiest of his life. After imitating a horse's whinny and a cow's moo, my two-year-old daughter Kate responds to the question, "And what does Pop say?" by imitating his belly laugh, "Whah, whah, whah." Despite the physical discomfort of his enforced inactivity and the endless patience it requires always to sit and wait for help, I think he is glad in the end that his suicide attempt failed.

With my father more adjusted to his blindness and the rest of the family moved in and rallied around him, I feel I have fulfilled the request my mother made of me at graduation. After nearly two years, it is finally time for graduate school. I will miss Gastonia more than I can imagine when I leave for Columbia in the spring of 1958. I will miss, terribly, my best-beloved buddies, Sid and Cora. Though I will visit often, visiting isn't the same as living with someone every day. I will miss my parents, my welfare clients, and even that hopeless old job itself.

Many mornings when I put on a white uniform to go to my part-time job as receptionist, secretary, quasi-nurse, and general "girl Friday" in a closed-up Madison Avenue physician's office, I think longingly of traveling to country sites in the black Gaston County sedan. I remember bare tree limbs against cloudless skies, like brush-strokes in Japanese paintings, and the magic of sunlight glistening on frosty fields. I can still see cows standing quietly in meadows making white clouds with their breath in the crisp morning air, and I can smell the fragrance of wood smoke mixed with that of clean sheets on the line by ten in the morning as I round the steep path to Mattie Smith's house on foot. I recall the pot of kidney beans already simmering on top of the wood-burning stove in the middle of her living room, and I can hear her say, "If you start them early, they'll be just right for supper, with collard greens and corn bread." That sounded good to me then, but it sounds even better on West 74th Street, where I share a room with hundreds of cockroaches, no matter how clean I keep the floor or how much I deprive us all of kidney bean and other fragrances. Being poor in New York doesn't feel the same as being poor in Gaston County. I'd take country poverty any day, but I have a mission in the city.

CHAPTER 2:

Viennese Psychoanalytic Psychiatry

N ew York is an exciting place for a country girl. Especially by contrast to the homogeneous South, it is a fascinating potpourri. Different nationalities, languages, cultures, and customs are squeezed against one another like grapes for a heady wine on this quite small island vineyard. Despite missing the green of growing things, which I never adjust to in New York, it has every other color and sensory stimulation imaginable. I never tire of walking through its ethnic neighborhoods. I walk a lot, and I think I walk through all of them. Until I find a job and begin a class at Columbia, I have little else to do.

I haunt the museums with which New York is so rich and the South so poor. I get lost in the Metropolitan with great regularity and pleasure. I especially love the Museum of Modern Art. After looking at the whole collection once, I divide my remaining time between Monet's water lilies and Picasso's goat. I eat lunch—or at least drink iced tea—in the sculpture garden as often as I can. In addition to sporting statuary animals, live pigeons and squirrels, it is also green. Once at the Guggenheim, where for some reason I am going *down* the ramp against the traffic, I run smack into Marlon Brando. Imagine that!

What a place Manhattan is—packed with people and with culture, yet astonishingly lonely. People don't talk to you as they do in the South. Finally, I find that part-time job and begin a night class at Columbia. Most of my fellow students swoop in for classes and out again as fast as they can. This is a commuter school with evening classes for people who work, and I never get to know anyone. A friend from Duke lives fairly close to me in the city. I visit her often, but she is married and pregnant, and as soon as her baby comes, our interests diverge and we drift apart.

After one spring and one summer semester at night school, where I have not made a single friend, I am trying to adjust to this fact, when suddenly the idea of switching from English to social work strikes me as a brilliant solution. I know Columbia has one of the best schools in the country. I also know it is housed in the old Carnegie Mansion on East 91st Street near the Metropolitan and the Guggenheim, and furthermore I know that it, like the Museum of Modern Art, has its own private garden. Primarily, however, I admit my real reason is, as a social worker, I will never be lonely. Talking is the social worker's business and, more or less, the clients have to respond. However, I am still only beginning to understand that my gravitating toward social work has something to do with the personal growth it forces me to face. I still struggle with my view that this field is beneath my dignity. I do not yet consider it a profession; instead, it is something a woman might occupy herself with while she waits for her real life to begin.

I am sophisticated enough to keep my attitudes about loneliness, partiality to green gardens, and my appraisal of social work out of my application essay. It never reveals a thing about these unusual reasons for applying, but I am not sophisticated enough to cover my tracks entirely. When the admissions' interviewer tests for ambivalence, she asks me why I have applied so late—in August—for fall classes. Unaware of the real reason for her question, I am genuinely alarmed and say, "But the course book says classes begin after Labor Day!" She laughs and graciously drops that line of questioning, or she might have pried loose those undesirable attitudes. But with two years of salary from Gaston County in my bank account, I do not need financial aid. I have more work experience than most candidates, and so, even as a tardy applicant, I am admitted. And my life does change dramatically.

At about this time, I do begin to notice an even more pronounced reversal in my perspective than I had recognized in my welfare work. Now I look deeply *inward* at the psychological architecture of myself and others. This has become habitual, and more importantly, by now, I understand its vital significance. I credit this outcome to my welfare job, and though I denigrate the source, I consider the product just short of a miracle. I also realize this depth of concentration will keep me oriented in the direction I have sought to go since as far back as my earliest memories take me.

What I don't recognize yet is that it is not the job that has restructured my vision. Not all people in this field look so closely at order and form in themselves and their clients. It is by the grace of God (in whom I don't believe) that I have been thus favored. And as I proceed on this course, it will bless me—or anyone else so oriented—exponentially as we live and grow, since as we live, oriented inwardly, we *will* grow psychologically. Later, I will also see that spiritual growth—which is truly what I longed for in childhood, but have now so adamantly disdained—follows psychological development as surely as daylight follows darkness.

Social work at Columbia far exceeds my expectations. I am right in assuming this "career" move will remedy my loneliness. Classes are exciting, and my fellow students are bright and energetic. Unlike night-school grads, this group is friendly. How else can they be? Also, we spend time together and share experiences. Social-work education is designed to promote sharing and relating. Two days a week, we are all on campus for classes in our mansion. We work in the library—a converted ballroom—and eat lunch on secluded garden benches. On wet or subzero days, we dine in the basement beside the train. A real train with real tracks once carried coal from the storage bin on one side of the building to the furnace on the other side, and, though it doesn't deliver coal any longer, it is still here.

On the remaining three school days, we report to our respective fieldwork placements. One of the truly great strengths of a social-work education is its fieldwork. Unlike training in psychology and psychiatry, where students do not encounter living clients until internship or residency, social-work students are plunged immediately into direct client contact. From the beginning, we assume responsibility for people. Closely supervised, the variety and volume of our work controlled, we practice classroom concepts with clients from the first week. Hands-on performance increases our anxiety as well as our camaraderie and our knowledge.

Six of us share a group placement at Manhattan State Hospital on Ward's Island. This island is in the East River between upper Manhattan and Queens. The Triborough Bridge, now the Kennedy Bridge, foots on it. Overshadowed by massive support pillars, three gray skyscrapers house the institution. You reach Manhattan State on a city bus that leaves from 125th Street and Fifth Avenue. We gather here on our first fieldwork morning, emerging from subway shafts or from the folding doors of buses. Though we have not met before, we know each other instantly. Quite different from everyone else on the street corner, we look spot-on "social-work school." We introduce ourselves as we wait for the bus. On that first morning, I meet Doug Roberts, who will become one of my closest friends. He is smoking a pipe and looking composed and totally in control, as he always looks, even though he isn't.

We also share one supervisor. Paid by the school and familiar with the setting, Gwendolyn Tyler is in her mid-fifties. She's been a social worker for decades and is an excellent teacher. We learn a lot from her and, of course, from our clients and from each other.

My first case is Lawrence Harrison. He is a young black man about my age who has been hospitalized for seven months. He came into the hospital hallucinating and is diagnosed schizophrenic. Now stabilized on antipsychotic medication, he is ready for discharge. My job is to facilitate this, to enlist the support of his family, to help him find work, and to reconnect socially. Lawrence is handsome, but he smiles too much. He has a false cheer and a wild look in his eyes that bespeaks how frightened he is, not only, I think, about rejoining society but of what his inner thoughts had been and perhaps still are at times. Also, it is truly unnerving to be on his ward. I have a fleeting moment of panic each time the guard lets me in and locks the door behind me. The first thing to assail my senses is the smell. In comparison to this, Etta's house *is* the florist shop she dreams of. Despite a fake pine scent, which makes it all the more sickening, the stench of urine is overpowering.

Once past the smell, the ward itself broadsides me. It is truly bedlam. One man obsessively paces an invisible rectangle. If he had a rifle on his shoulder, and a tall bear-skin helmet, he could be changing the guard in front of Buckingham Palace. Maybe he thinks he is. Another yells out loudly every now and again for an attendant. Otherwise, he lies listlessly on his cot. No one comes, at least while I am there. Another man, trembling with anxiety, accosts everyone who enters his field of vision, including me, to affirm that he is in the right place. And what is this place? And when is lunch?

I immediately empathize with Lawrence. He is pleased to meet me. He extends himself, making it quite clear he'll take all the help he can get—to get *out* of here, and *home*. We discuss his past employment. Maybe his old boss at the convenience store will want him back, but he'll take anything. When high school comes up, he confesses he hasn't graduated. School is hard for him. He isn't interested, but he'll try again if his parents and I think it is a good idea. He has no friends, was always isolated, living with his parents on 134th street and staying close to home. His four siblings are older, and he was never particularly close with them. Without hesitation, Lawrence gives me permission to visit his parents. Both of us agree I should arrange our next meeting off the ward in the coffee shop on the ground floor. I will escort him down on Friday. In the meantime, I will try to see his parents and contact his former boss. Lawrence smiles less rigidly as we shake hands on this bargain. I am the first tangible proof he's had that he may be on his way home. I meet with his parents the following day.

"You told them *what*?" Gwendolyn looks up from my notes of that interview in alarm. These are the days when it is *verboten* to disclose the name a doctor has attached to his patient's condition, but I don't know that.

"I told them his diagnosis. I thought they should know. How can they cooperate with his outpatient treatment if they don't know what's wrong with him?"

Gwendolyn pales. Her brow furrows. Her eyes narrow. Her hands shake. She is struggling hard not to lose control and scream at me. "You just told those people that their son has the worst disease known to mankind! That is devastating. It doesn't do them any good to know what you *call* it. That can only make them worry. What they need is a working description of his problem."

Later I learn that Gwendolyn herself has a schizophrenic son. But all I can think now is that maybe I should become an English professor after all. *Loneliness isn't so bad, and social work may have been a grim mistake, but the Harrison's hadn't seemed so upset. Maybe they hadn't had time to react. By now they could be in cardiac arrest.*

"Well, what can I do?" I ask.

"Damage control. From now on describe their son's problems. Talk on that level about how they can help him. Tell them Lawrence is very shy and vulnerable. He has many fears, like a young child has. He needs gentle support and encouragement, but he shouldn't be overprotected either." She recovers her composure before I recover mine.

"In some cases, the parents of schizophrenics are inconsistent. They do not understand how to strike a good balance between being protective and at the same time encouraging their child to experience and to master his own feelings. They may err in both directions. This is what you need to watch for, one pattern or the other, or both. If you see these behaviors, then you can help the Harrisons with them."

Lawrence's former boss is a family friend who agrees to give him a job delivering takeout orders, and soon Lawrence is discharged to live at home. I continue to work with the Harrisons and with Lawrence during the next eight months of that school year. Lawrence does well on his medication, and his parents always receive me graciously and seem genuinely interested in doing all they can to help their son.

Gwendolyn is right. The Harrisons do overprotect

Lawrence, particularly socially. He has always been sensitive and easily rejected, they tell me, frequently returning from school in tears. Lawrence, his parents, and I meet with Reverend Jones, their pastor, and with Mrs. Sparks, the social director at the First Baptist Church, where the Harrison's have long been members. We talk about Lawrence's shyness and his need for support with peers. Mrs. Sparks offers to introduce him to a young man and his sister who are new church members. They can attend her social club and support each other.

When I leave my student placement at year's end, Lawrence is more relaxed and comfortable. Socializing is still difficult for him, but he is letting people help him over some of the rough spots. For the first time, he reports feeling legitimate as a member of a social group. This is certainly a simple intervention, but I am relieved that whatever initial mistakes I made weren't fatal.

Soon after beginning work with Lawrence, Gwendolyn assigns Rosanna Rodriguez to me. Rosanna is also diagnosed schizophrenic, but she doesn't have any parents, at least not in the U.S. Her parents are in Puerto Rico. Rosanna has been raised in the States by an elderly aunt and uncle. When I meet her, I see that the description "attractive" is totally inadequate to describe Rosanna. She is unbelievably beautiful. Like Lawrence, she is about my age, and, also like him, she is stabilized on medication and ready for discharge. Again, my job is to help her in practical ways to reenter her community and resume normal living.

When she leaves the hospital, I accompany her

home. As we walk down 125th Street to the room she rents in her relatives' apartment, every man and most of the women turn just to look at Rosanna.

"How do you stand it?" I ask. "I never understood before that being beautiful could be a curse. I mean all that attention is flattering, but it's so intrusive. You don't have any privacy. It's practically like being a movie star."

She smiles one of her show-stopping smiles. She is glad I notice and can understand. "I pretend it isn't happening, but that's not healthy. Usually I wear a wedding ring. That helps some. But I lost the one I was using."

"Maybe you should wear a ski mask or become a Muslim like Malcolm X. You might be safe behind a burka or a caftan."

She laughs. "Let's go in here. I've been hungry for tripe for months."

"What's tripe?"

"You've never had tripe?"

"I never even heard of it."

"It's the lining of a cow's stomach. It doesn't sound appetizing, but it's very good." She points to one of the trays in the butcher's shop. It is filled with slabs of yellowish blubber. One side appears to be smooth, and the other is porous with openings about the size of fish eye sockets.

"You eat that? I've instantly become a vegetarian, myself."

She laughs again. This is a good sign. She has continued coming to life in the several weeks I have known her. She has lost the dingy skin tone that had somewhat diminished her beauty in the beginning of our contact. Now, and particularly when she laughs, she is radiant.

Ignoring the four people ahead of us, the butcher practically falls on his knife as he hastens to serve Rosanna. Men can be such idiots sometimes. He languishes over counting out her change, carefully placing each coin in Rosanna's upturned palm. Then he comes from behind the counter to hold the door for us. Meanwhile, none of the other customers, even in this city, make any complaint. Rosanna has also mesmerized them.

"I'm taking you with me whenever I go shopping," I say. "New York might just be manageable with a face like yours." She laughs.

"I see the drawbacks, all right, but there are definite advantages. Forget the ski mask," I joke. "We'll just have to make do."

Rosanna gets her old job back as a seamstress for a tailor. Her room is oppressive. Her aunt and uncle are themselves depressed and depressing. They are old and sick and crotchety. I think Rosanna should move. She is afraid. She says it isn't safe out there.

Whenever I go to visit Rosanna, I have to traverse one of Harlem's dense crime districts. Mine is usually the only white face on the street. However, I do not feel frightened, at least not for more than a few fleeting moments every now and again, when a particularly unsavory-looking character appears to be eyeing me specifically. Every time that happens I long for Mrs. Harris' yellow dog, Buster. I could use his particular talents just now. I am never fearful when a client accompanies me. Even alone, I know I look the part of a social worker, in the same way we six students had looked to each other on that first morning at the bus stop. Clearly I have business here and so, in a certain way, I belong. For the most part, people don't give me a second glance.

Things go well for Rosanna until after Christmas. Sometime in January, I notice a little of that old dullness creeping back into her face. I ask what is wrong. She says she has cut down on her medication.

"Well, it shows," I say. "I don't want you to get sick again. You don't want to go back to the hospital, do you?"

Her beautiful eyes fill with tears. "No, but I do want to be myself. The medicine isn't me."

"Now what do I do?" I ask Gwendolyn, who has finally forgiven me for my initial blunder with the Harrisons. "She has been going to group therapy every week and seeing me, but I'm not a therapist, and I suspect she's not taking *any* medication."

"We can get her a medication consult, and we can ask for individual therapy," Gwendolyn says without much enthusiasm. I know she's dubious about our chances for success, and she is right. Nothing works for Rosanna this time around, and, in the spring, she returns to the hospital, where her Thorazine is increased, and we talk a lot about her feeling inauthentic.

"I'd rather have bad feelings than no feelings at all," she says gravely.

I ask her about losing her parents at the age of three. Does she remember feeling more real in Puerto Rico? She describes early memories of music and dancing and laughter. She remembers something else, too—something dark and ugly—but she can't recall details.

"Could that have been about leaving your parents and your own tropical birthplace to come to New York?" I wonder, knowing full-well how depressing such a major life change can be, even for an adult. She knows she's never liked New York. She is not even sure why she was sent. Her aunt and uncle say it is because of better schools and because her parents are poor, but we get no clarity about her dark memory. We can agree that, while the medicine doesn't help it, that inauthentic feeling is probably not solely due to Thorazine. The feeling didn't dissipate when she took herself off her medication entirely. We are beginning to get underneath the surface, behind some of Rosanna's defenses, and I feel, despite my lack of training, that we are close to some real and important therapeutic work, but we don't have enough time. I will go to a different placement next year. I hope she can eventually remember more from her past and work on her depression in the individual therapy that Gwendolyn and I have so strongly recommended. In the meantime, I am learning a little about therapy from classes and from interactions like this.

My third client, Abe Golden, is from Brooklyn, a so-called advantaged neighborhood. He is a diminutive man in his fifties, an insurance salesman. He is recovering from his second major depressive episode. Abe also needs help reentering his community, which is a formidable task indeed, since his community consists of a tight alliance between his wife Eva and their twenty-eight-year-old son Harvey. Emotionally, Abe has been excluded from this family unit for years, and, as far as I can tell, so is everyone else, including Harvey's new wife.

"Eva will expect me to go back to work, and I don't feel ready," Abe says as he wrings his hands and moves nervously in his chair. His mouth trembles as if he might cry, and I wonder if he's ever said no to Eva in his life. When I meet her, I better understand.

Like her husband, Eva is physically small, but her presence fills a room, and Abe shrinks to accommodate her. She crackles with energy like a snapped high voltage wire. She is pretty, smart, and efficient. Powerfully, she transmits the message that she, and she alone, knows the truth of all things. I can see why Abe feels intimidated, and I haven't even met Harvey yet.

On our second visit to his home, Harvey is there with his mother. He is a chiropractor, "and very successful, too," he quickly lets me know. "As a matter of fact," he adds, "You look as though you could use an adjustment right now. Have you ever had one? No? Chiropractics is very popular in the South." He goes on to inform me that adjustments are really quite simple. You must be trained to hold the patient's arms and neck just so, he demonstrates loosely on his mother, and to apply the right amount of pressure. "Then, snap!" he says gleefully. "That cracking sound in the neck releases all the tension and soreness. You feel like a new person, believe me!" I am thankful that I don't have to refuse a free treatment. Harvey is causing enough trouble as it is.

He is plainly wired to his mother, and the two of them form an invincible force, modeling the dyad defined at school. I move my seat closer to Abe, who sits hunched on a floral-print couch. The red of the large rose in repeating bouquets matches that of Eva's dress. If you don't match Eva, like me and Abe, what else can you do in this place but become depressed? In our tiny corner, I try to carry on a lame conversation with Abe. It isn't going anywhere. *What would Gwendolyn advise*? Desperate, I go for broke.

"Harvey, don't you have a home of your own?"

"Why, yes, I married last year. We had to conduct the wedding around Abe's second depressive episode! He almost ruined it."

Harvey is very aggressively retaking the offensive, but I am not giving up so easily. Instead I charge ahead. At least Abe and I are in the conversation now.

"Your parents need this time *alone* to talk about your father's coming home." Abe is on a weekend pass to test how things might go. Not well, by my current assessment.

"Well?" he sputters, as if reading my thoughts, and, "*Well!*" as if quite a little dampened by the cold water I've thrown in his direction. "*My* mother," emphasis on "my" noted, "has a right to some support. It's been very hard for her to take over everything, to be both breadwinner and housewife."

I am willing to give most people the benefit of the doubt, but I can't buy this. *Eva doesn't appear to have had trouble taking over anything. In fact, I think she'll have trouble letting go*, but I try diplomacy. Turning to her, I say, "I'm sure it has been hard for you."

"Frankly, I doubt that Abe *can* get better," she says

with real malevolence. I see Abe purse his trembling lips. Coming from her, doubts of success sound like definitive outcome predictions, but she does lower the voltage a little.

Again, I have to ask Harvey to leave so that his parents and I can talk. I say it is my job to support them both. Eva telegraphs that he can go. Though minor, this temporary energy shift feels major to me. I request that we focus on their problems as a couple. At least they are talking, and I have effected that change. *Maybe there is hope for me after all.*

Back at the hospital, Gwendolyn uses the Goldens' situation to teach me something about Freud's then-dominant oedipal theory. "Especially if parents have not resolved their own oedipal issues, they are likely to repeat them unconsciously with their own children," she says. "This sounds a lot like what's going on with your 'dynamic duo.'

"Simply put, the oedipal conflict appears at the point in a young child's life before she, in Eva's case, knows that she can move beyond the original infant-mother dyad to include another person as an intimate love object. Including a third person is very frightening for someone who has only experienced dyads. They fear, of course, that losing one is losing all. With no concept of triads, relationships *are* all or nothing.

"Freud observed that children three to five years old were able to discriminate gender and to notice the connection between couples, yet they remained emotionally enmeshed in dyads. Without knowing they might add a third, oedipal children feel they have to love one parent and reject the other. Freud saw them forming intense attachments with their opposite-sex parents. But the result was unstable and uncomfortable, 'ambivalently held' by the child who really needs and loves both parents. This developmental moment poses a true psychic crisis.

"Freud thought that the resolution of the conflict was different for the two sexes. He said boys give up their rivalry with their fathers out of fear. Bottom line, according to Freud, is the boy's fantasy that his father will castrate him if he doesn't back off his mother-attachment and identify with his father. A healthy boy does just that and resigns himself to fulfilling his wish for intimacy sometime in the future with a partner of his own. Freud calls this resignation 'sublimation.' He also thought girls never resolved their oedipal conflicts because they were 'castrated' already, so there was no motivation to give anything up."

I could hardly believe my ears. *What an outrage!* Of course, I myself had felt a lot of rivalry with men, especially since my mother clearly favored my older brother *because* he was male. Gwendolyn must see smoke coming out of my ears, as she quickly adds, "Don't look so grim, a modern theorist named Edith Jacobson has reconciled gender development. She makes a good case for both sexes resolving the oedipal complex in the same way, motivated by *love* for both parents, instead of by fear. In any case, when and if the child does resolve this issue, then the developmental sun shines, and he or she moves beyond exclusivity and into the warm understanding that love and intimacy can include more than one person at a time," Gwendolyn concludes with mock irony.

Admittedly corny, but somewhat informative, that

explanation does nothing to reverse the fact that Freud and his oedipal theory are still taught and still prevail as "revealed truth" in the world of psychiatry. The theory is not only personally offensive, it offends me intellectually as well.

"How can a theory of human development get away with looking at boys and girls so *differently*?" I ask, inadvertently revealing my own female oedipal envy, that I had known about forever. Gwendolyn kindly passes up the opportunity to interpret my remark and so nail my Freudian doubt with a lethal comment. She adds simply that she thinks girls and boys *are* different, in their heads as well as in their bodies. Teasingly, she quotes that old saw, "'Biology is destiny,' you know."

Though I want to argue the point—throw in a few questions about culture and gender education—I don't. Instead, I make a mental note: *Attention needed: BIG theoretical problem here.* I feel certain there is a missing piece somewhere that will allow this theory to apply to everyone; that is, if it is a valid theory and if psychology is a valid science. At this time, most people don't think so. Instead, psychology is considered an art. Unlike physics, mathematics, biology, etc., psychology has no laws but is a loosely bound set of anecdotes and developmental patterns like this one called "the oedipal complex." With that as your theoretical support, you must be artful, indeed, to relieve a client suffering from conflict. Despite knowing my own feelings and understanding that some aspects of the theory had validity, I felt it needed balance to make it work equally well for both sexes before it could come close to being "scientifically" acceptable. Imbalanced thinking like this is *dangerous*. It makes human behavior chaotic. In the meantime, I have to grab anything I can get my hands on to address my immediate problem in Brooklyn.

"So how does all this apply to the Goldens?" I ask.

"Like many people, perhaps like most people," Gwendolyn replies, "the Goldens can't resolve their ambivalence about each other. They think in dyads. They can't imagine loving a second person without losing the one they've got. Emotional immaturity is like medieval geography. Since you can't see over the horizon, the world is flat from wherever you stand, and, if you try to move on to the next more advanced position, you will fall off the edge into never-ending space. Unable to resolve their dilemma, the Goldens play favorites. Clinging to mutually exclusive attachments is one of the most common causes of problems in relationships. The Goldens are an especially vivid example. You're lucky. It's a good case to learn from."

Having already experienced their interaction in shockingly electrical terms, it isn't that hard to see the dilemma. "So Eva can't love both Abe *and* Harvey. Harvey can't love both Eva *and* Abe. Abe can't love *anybody* because they won't *let* him, so he just gets *depressed*."

"That sounds about right."

"But it sounds hopeless. What on earth can I do with that?"

"It's not necessarily hopeless. You have to remember, as strong as their fear of changing may be, their discomfort at being out of balance is even stronger. Continue what you started, breaking up those exclusive dyads. Meet with Abe and Eva. Meet with Abe and Harvey, if that should prove useful, but *don't* meet with Eva and Harvey alone, and especially avoid meeting with all of them together just now. Harvey and Eva won't let you in, and if you try, Harvey and his mother will gang up against you and Abe again. When you can, ask Eva about her relationship with her own father. I have a feeling she was a 'daddy's girl' and felt either guilt because she was her father's favorite or longing toward her mother, whom she felt had rejected her because, as Eva knew only too well, her own feelings toward her mother were rarely kind. In fact, my bet is that Eva was intensely jealous and envious of her mother, as oedipal daughters are.

"In the present," Gwendolyn continues, "Eva reverses the roles, but she repeats the drama. In her unconscious, Harvey probably represents herself when she was a child. She and Harvey are both 'making it up' to Mom and at the same time getting a kick out of their 'illicit' parent/ child relationship. Abe is the 'one too many' whom they both want out of the way. To them, on a conscious level, his job was over when he fathered Harvey, but unconsciously he's still necessary to keep the triangle interesting."

It is a lot to take in, but I can relate to it myself. If Eva were a daddy's girl, and both she and I harbored guilty longings for our mothers and felt deprived of her love, then neither of us could have very good self-esteem. It is clear why my mother hadn't loved me enough. I lost out in a "male-centric" society because I was female. Whatever Eva's reason for needing to skew intimate relationships, it is probably accompanied by some sense of her own defectiveness.

To paraphrase George Santayana, unless we remember it, history will repeat itself. This is an especially dangerous truth in the psyche, where repression can highjack memory and create a permanent kind of "forgetting," making repetition a certainty. Freud called this the "repetition compulsion." Here's where "the sins of our fathers" made more dynamic sense, and I could better understand some of the senseless impediments to their basic quality of life that my welfare clients had first shown me.

I arrange an interview with Eva. We talk about her background. She does, in fact, idealize her father, and she assists him in the small store he operates throughout the Depression. Her mother dies of pneumonia before Eva goes to school, and she feels her mother's loss more acutely through her father's palpable grief than because she herself holds strong feelings of loss. She serves as her father's right hand, hurrying home from school to relieve him at the counter. She never imagines that she will marry and feels contented as an "old maid." When Abe comes along, her father encourages her to accept his proposal. Eva suspects that he has "arranged" her marriage quietly by persuading Abe of its merits. Soon after the wedding, Eva's father dies and she is inconsolable.

It is not until she becomes pregnant and has a son of her own that Eva begins to take an interest in life again. During those days, for the first time, Eva feels love for Abe. He is a good father to Harvey and loyal and loving to Eva. In these respects, he reminds her of her own father. Harvey is a demanding baby and takes most of Eva's time. Gradually, she tells me, Abe just fades into the background, and they both allow it to happen. She is shocked when he first becomes clinically depressed and has to be hospitalized. She must admit, however, that she is scornful of what she considers a *defect* and that she looses what little respect she has left for him.

"Perhaps that's when you *really* shut him out?"

"I guess I did, but how could I feel supportive when my father had been through so much more pain without giving in to it?"

"You know, people express their feelings in very different ways. Maybe your father was able to 'put his grief to work,' so to speak. That has definite advantages. However, no one knows better than you how much constant pain he lived with."

"I think it killed him, frankly. I think as soon as he saw me married, he gave in to it and died of his grief for my mother." Eva says, crying now. These feelings are extremely difficult for her to reexperience.

When her tears subside, I say, "You are probably entirely right about your father, but Abe *can* talk about his grief. And fortunately the one he grieves for is still *alive* to hear his feelings. When Harvey was young, you felt love and respect for Abe. Maybe you can again. I know he loves you. Talk to him, and let him talk to you. That is the most effective medicine ever devised."

Maybe Eva and Abe are on their way toward resolving some of their problems, but my field work is coming to a close, and I have to leave them here. I never forget, however, that seeing Eva's problems helps me focus my own similar ones more clearly. Though I will work on them in a personal analysis and later in therapy, most of the insight that helps me with resolution comes from life experience with clients and in my own significant relationships. It will be another ten years before I feel a major self-esteem shift.

At my evaluation, Gwendolyn says, "You've come a long way this year. You are beginning to understand what psychotherapy is all about. Where will you request a placement next year?"

"I don't know," I answer. "It doesn't look good for getting into a psychiatric setting in New York. Most of the second-year placements are in adoption agencies and nursing homes. That doesn't sound very dynamic, though it could be OK, if I got a great supervisor." Gwendolyn smiles, acknowledging my compliment.

"The student grapevine claims that Boston offers many more options for psychiatric social-work placements. Some of us think we might transfer to Simmons."

"Let me know if I can use my influence to get you into a good program. The school and the professors—classwork altogether, for that matter—are less important than your fieldwork," Gwendolyn confirms my own conclusion. Without experience, theories remain ideas as opposed to knowledge. The most vital learning always takes place in the present tense. I will appreciate this exponentially as time goes by.

I do transfer to Simmons and move to Boston. If social work restored people to my life, Boston restores greenery. The Simmons School of Social Work is at 51 Commonwealth Avenue, and the brownstone dwellings along this street each have small front lawns. Every lawn has its own magnolia tree, so in the spring when they bloom, Commonwealth Avenue is a showplace. In addition, the broad lanes of Back Bay's major thoroughfare are separated by a beautiful mall, itself planted with trees, grass, and flowers. The mall is part of the 1,100-acre chain of nine parks and waterways that ring the city and include the Fenway, the Boston Garden, the Boston Common, the Muddy River, and my two favorites, Jamaica Pond and Arnold Arboretum. All of this is the Emerald Necklace designed at the turn of the century by Frederick Law Olmsted, the great landscape architect who also designed Central Park in New York City.

Boston suits me very well, with a reasonable blend of city life and natural beauty. I feel at home here as I had not in New York. Furthermore, that all-important field placement for which I have moved to Boston, even without any of the other benefits, turns out to be well worth the trouble. It is at the Beth Israel Hospital's Child Guidance Clinic.

The entire psychiatric department of the Beth Israel is the new stronghold of the prestigiously trained and recently displaced analysts from Freud's former sanctum sanctorum, Vienna. The name itself elicits shockwaves of reverence throughout Boston's psychiatric community, and the Beth Israel has the reputation of being the hottest training spot in town. What I don't know is that, in addition to all its advertised assets, the BI's most valuable commodity will turn out to be my supervisor, Anne Gerber. She supervises all the Simmons social-work students at the hospital, just as Gwendolyn does for the Columbia students at Manhattan State.

I meet Anne on the first day of my second-year-fieldwork placement. She is about 5'4" tall with red hair that is graying slightly. She wears it simply blunt cut and her glasses are plain gold-framed and serviceable. Her clothing is also simple, basic, carefully chosen for quality without concern for style. Her shoes are the kind that old ladies wear. They lace up and have fat, medium-height heels. Anne dresses as though to prevent the stuff of the superficial world from draining an ounce of attention from her focus on a higher plane. Her whole demeanor, especially her face, expresses kindness, gentleness, peace, and tranquility. She speaks in a low voice, slowly and thoughtfully, with an ever-so-slight Eastern European accent. She is clearly very intelligent, very learned, and very wise. Most of all she exudes that her being is about teaching. Later someone tells me that Anne is a Solovechek. For centuries, her family have been rabbis and scholars in the ghettos of Eastern Europe. They are highly respected for their learning and their wisdom. Why am I not surprised?

One of my first assignments at the Beth Israel is to evaluate Eric Stern's parents. Anne prepares her students for this first set of interviews, but nothing can prepare one for the unexpected, which every client is. Moreover, each person who comes for help has been carefully preparing for years to grab at relief from painful symptoms; but also, like Eva, frightened that letting go will be self-destructive, each is also preparing to resist that change with uncanny cunning.

Eric does poorly in school, and though he is a fourth-grader, he still wets his bed. For recently immigrated and upwardly mobile families, as we presume the Sterns to be, bed-wetting is tolerated, but poor grades are not. When I meet with these parents, I learn that grades are, indeed, the leading problem in their minds—even though Eric is described as a demanding child, who never allows his parents to leave him with a sitter and who refuses to go to bed unless one of his parents promises to sleep with him. The separation problem and the bed-wetting ignored, Mr. Stern launches right into poor grades. He tells me that when Eric first brought home failing marks, he immediately intervened at school. He met with his son's teacher and accused her of being prejudiced against Jews. When he learns that she herself is Jewish, he simply says he's known a lot of Jews who are prejudiced against Jews, but he lets the topic go. Since then, he reviews Eric's homework nightly, rewriting it all himself after Eric and his mother go to bed. Then, waking the child in the morning, he supervises his son's recopying of the corrected papers so they can be passed in at school as Eric's work.

"That's a lot of effort for all of you, Mr. Stern, but Eric's tests at school show he's not gaining much from it. Might there be a better way?" I ask, still incredulous at what I have just heard. *How could anyone conceive such a strategy?*

"Are you suggesting that I let him fail? What kind of person are you? You work in a child guidance clinic, but you don't care about children!"

Outwardly, I maintain my composure, or so I think. I say, "Eric scores well on intelligence tests. Maybe he can learn to do his own work. I know you love your son, Mr. Stern, and I know you want him to succeed." I wade right in and continue, "I'm just questioning your approach because it doesn't seem to be working."

"Don't you criticize me, young lady. You have plenty of problems yourself. Your cheek is twitching. You have a tic! That's a psychiatric disorder, a serious one."

I know a tic is serious, and I know I don't have one. What Mr. Stern observes is probably the palpitation of my carotid artery. Anxiety makes my heart race, and anywhere an artery shows just under the skin, it reveals the pounding of my way over-stimulated heart. Temples I know about, cheeks I haven't noticed before. Nonplussed, I say, "We are here to discuss Eric's problems, not mine, Mr. Stern." This man is only one of my tough new customers. They are not the blatant, in-your-face, physically challenging sort of client like Jude from Gaston County, but in their own wily ways they are much more challenging. Even so, I feel sorry for Eric. His father is an angry man.

"Frightened," Anne instructs. "Think. How did he make you feel?"

"Threatened," I reply. "I had no idea what to do. It was an important moment. I should have said something therapeutic, but all I could think of was getting out of there."

"What you did was fine," Anne tries to reassure me. "To turn those moments into effective therapy, you need to know that what you felt was countertransference.

Mr. Stern evoked in you the feelings he himself felt and projected onto you. The best defense being a good offense in football as well as in psychiatry, he threw everything he had at you. Believe it or not, his anxiety was greater than yours, and the whole process was unconscious to him. He really thought all the anxiety in the room belonged to you.

"Another term you should know is Anna Freud's 'identification with the aggressor.' In Mr. Stern's eyes, you held all the power in that interview. You could reduce him to ashes before his wife, so he turned the tables on you. He 'became' what he envisioned you to be.

"You can respond to such a maneuver with trained empathy. Speak directly to his unconscious and say something like, 'Mr. Stern, we are both doing fine. Blaming each other, or blaming Eric, won't get our work done. We're both on the same side here, Eric's side. If we're going to help him, we need to work together.' Phrases such as 'doing fine,' 'same side,' 'no blame,' and 'working together' go a long way with such a man, desperate to prove his value by material and numerical success."

At case conferences, with all of Vienna watching, I am expected to perform at a high standard. Just sitting at one of those formal conferences, never mind presenting a case, is enough to give me terminal anxiety. I develop a new symptom. For the first time in my life, speaking before that group, I stammer. There's nothing to do for that problem but to prepare well, to overprepare, in writing. If I can resort to reading, at least I won't stumble over my words and look like I belong on the anxiety disorder unit.

I sweat and blush and stammer my way through that training year at the BI. I curse myself plenty for leaving New York, even for leaving North Carolina. I seem to have a propensity for putting myself in the kitchen without being at all sure I can stand the heat. But gradually I begin to feel more sure of myself on this abstract psychic landscape. By now, I can look back at my Welfare clients and know Jude is a psychopath and both Etta Mae and Billy Ray are "Passive Narcissistic Characters" who belong in Piaget's Stage II of very early development, with the emotional structure of a child of 1 to 4 months old.

At this time, social workers are responsible for working with parents. Child guidance is just becoming an "in" thing, and only psychiatrists, with medical degrees, are allowed to work with children. Thank God. Adults are so much more complex and interesting, and I learn a lot from working with them. Though they clearly make me anxious at times, I get further confirmation that we all learn best when experience enlivens concepts.

Christine and John Sullivan are Tony's parents. Referred by a team of pediatricians who have carefully ruled out physical causes, the Sullivans bring their six-year-old son to the clinic. Tony's doctors conjecture that instead of expressing feelings when upset, Tony spikes fevers. This is an unusual symptom, so the Sullivans are a big deal around the clinic, another "interesting" case. There are long discussions at case conferences about whether or not fevers *can* be induced by emotions. How would such a physiological mechanism *work?* Is it related to seizures? If so, how? No one has written about this phenomenon.

Perhaps Dr. Cochran, Tony's therapist, can write a paper. As the parent therapist, I get a lot of conference exposure from Tony's fevers.

As usual, when children have symptoms, their parents have marital problems. Tony is the Sullivans' first of five children. Christine enjoys being a mother, but in her solo interview she tells me that she is troubled by the tension in her home. John works long hours as an automobile mechanic and comes home too late and too tired to help with childcare, but he insists that Christine apply his methods in his absence. Christine feels John is "autocratic," like his own father, whom John feared and avoided as a child, while he looked to his mother for protection. Christine thinks John is acting like his father and pushing her to play the protector as his mother did with him. The Sullivans argue often. I sympathize with Christine. Anne has to remind me about countertransference. She wants me to see the family from John's perspective, too.

John is an earnest young man, a conscientious worker, eager to please his boss. Unable to control his temper in adolescence, he was always fighting with someone, verbally with teachers, physically with peers. He was a poor student, as though his mind were always nursing a grudge and never free for learning. He felt excluded by his father, who idolized his younger brother. As an adult, John still feels devalued, because his wife dotes on the children, leaving him, once again, out in the cold. Feeling helpless, he resorts to his adolescent attack strategy.

As I work with the Sullivans, Anne helps me to identify the very simple pattern in Tony's fevers. They occur when his parents quarrel, quite often just at his bedtime when John usually comes in from work, and occasionally before a big test in school. When Tony has a fever, the usual family routines are suspended. John backs off his hard-nosed stance and relieves Christine of her routine duties so she can sit with Tony, who only allows his mother to comfort him.

One day during a gale-force blizzard when only she and I make it into the officially "closed" clinic, Christine confesses, "While Tony is sick and I am sitting beside him in that quiet, dark room, holding a damp cloth to his forehead, I am happy. Isn't that terrible?" she asks in a barely audible whisper. "I'm actually happy when my son is sick."

This time I feel more sure of how to respond. "Terrible? Not at all. Look at what you've been telling me: You and John don't understand each other. You try to make your lives mesh even though you see things from different perspectives. When you drop your defensive stances with each other, you cooperate and your home runs smoothly. Right now Tony's fevers create that atmosphere. You'll just have to learn to do the same thing without depending on him to elicit family harmony."

"Oh," she says. Christine is learning from what she has just told me. And so it goes, until the Sullivans can see each other without the distorting lenses of the past and Tony no longer needs his fevers to get their love.

Family dynamics are very interesting. Since I know that every psychic structure is based on two opposing drives or urges, in a troubled family, each parent seems to play out one or the other drive "role." This balances the collective psyche. The "problem" child cements the arrangement, creating stasis and stalemate. Like Tony's fever, the child's symptom reflects and reveals the underlying family drama and it's resolution usually brings relief.

The Dupuises are a particularly dramatic illustration of unresolved individual drives intermeshing and temporarily sustaining each other in an unhealthy family system. Theirs is another high-profile case.

In the 1960s, long before incest was discovered to be much more than a Freudian fantasy, Lavonne, fourteen, and Sylvia, eleven, come to the clinic. And though, in retrospect, perhaps Rosanna and other people I know are also victims, Lavonne and Sylvia are the first two children I meet with documented histories of incest. I also meet their mother and their father, the perpetrator. Though jarred, our clinic staff manages the people involved and the immediate community adroitly, with compassion, understanding, and delicacy. It is not easy in the days when such matters are neither disclosed nor handled as often as they are today.

We speculate about this family at an intake conference when new assignments are being made, and we pool our meager knowledge. We know Mrs. Dupuis is a very disturbed woman. During an admission for minor surgery, she has revealed the incest to our medical staff. While suffering a dissociative episode or flashback, she describes the event as if it is happening before her eyes. If their mother is so ill, then what kind of sickness can we expect to see in their father, now on probation, charged with incest and living outside the home, permitted to see his children only on supervised visits? How can these children be functioning at all?

And they *are* functioning. They go to school, and Lavonne does quite well there. Sylvia has trouble keeping up and paying attention in class, but still she is learning at a modest rate. A grandmother lives close by and is involved with the children, but it is she who raised their father.

Mrs. Dupuis is definitely pathetic. She is almost unable to care for herself. She can barely keep her mind focused during an interview, and she frequently stops talking, lost, it appears, in fantasy. If I ask what she is thinking, she says something like, "Oh, nothing. Nothing much. I can't remember now..." She lets me know that, for all his ills, she relies on her husband to organize the family and on Lavonne, too. I conclude that Lavonne is, functionally, the mother in this household and that Mr. Dupuis is more child than coparent. It is Lavonne who had the most sustained sexual relationship with her father. Sylvia, disorganized and distracted, identifies more with her mother and is more like her mother. She reports only a few sexual encounters.

Mr. Dupuis does not deny his guilt. He won't or can't explain it either. "It began when Elaine was so sick that she couldn't have me sleep in the same bed with her. I moved to the living-room couch. Lavonne would come to sit there when she awoke from a bad dream. It just happened. At first I only touched her. Then it became something more." He puts his head down and sobs. He seems genuinely grieved. "Now I hardly ever see them. I know that's the way it has to be, but their mother isn't well enough to care for them. I can only hope my mother fills in."

Anne wants me to work with Lavonne. "She needs a female therapist. She is fourteen and, therefore, almost an adult. Don't look like you just saw a ghost. It'll be fine. We can talk about your sessions before and after each one if necessary."

Lavonne is a very pretty girl. She is crisp, all business, hardly like any fourteen-year-old I'd ever met. She tells her story better than either parent can tell their own, but despite her competence as a client, I am very uncomfortable with her. I think this might be because I have never worked with a child before. Then I realize I feel more lonely than frightened in her presence. I feel quite isolated, as though this competent businesswoman is relating to me through a locked and bolted door.

As agreed, Anne gives me extra supervision. She thinks my feelings when I am with Lavonne are countertransferential. Despite the grown-up façade she presents," Anne thinks, "Lavonne must feel very lonely inside.

"That's the kind of protective facade that many children with boundariless parents construct. In fact, it's the favorite defense of the 'parentified child' who has had to reverse roles with their parents from early on. Lavonne may have nurtured her parents rather than the other way around for more years than I'd care to imagine. Her mother just isn't there, and her father is much too present. We can bet that underneath the facade that tells you to keep your distance, lives Lavonne's own deeply bereft and deeply needy version of her parents, and that core self has a lot of intense feelings."

It is many months before Lavonne lets me in on

anything so personal as a feeling, intense or not. Slowly and painstakingly, we grope our way toward some emotional contact with each other. Then, one day, she drops her facade.

"Ya know, you say you care about me, and that we can work together, but I didn't want to come here today! You *made* me come! 'It's our time, Lavonne, and we can't let anything interfere with that,'" she mimics what I had said on the phone when she had called earlier to cancel her appointment.

"Well, it's not *my* time! It's *your* fucking time! I wanted to play basketball with my friends!" she weeps. "And you were the one who said I should make friends, get out of the house, *enjoy* my childhood! You're full of shit, Morrison, and I'm taking off right now!"

I don't know what would have happened if the door handle in that temporary, prefabricated cubicle we called an office hadn't fallen off as she leapt on it, but it does, and we both crack up. She has finally told me something with real feeling: she "hates me and wants out," and suddenly here she is locked up with me for who knows how long. It is late on a Friday afternoon, and the clinics usually held in the area are closed, the corridors deserted.

Of course, it isn't really a crisis. We have a working telephone, and I call security to explain our predicament. I know that, worst case, we can walk right through these walls which are not much more sturdy than the door fittings. When I say this to Lavonne, she looks more comfortable; in fact, she smiles at the thought of walking through the walls.

In the magical psychological moments while we wait for the guard to let us out, Lavonne lets me in on her deepest secret. She wants to be close to someone, but the price has always been too high. She can't do it. She feels she is locked inside herself, and she is in torment. She wants to be loved desperately, desperately enough to have sex with her father, even though she knows it isn't right, but she *can't* have emotional closeness, ever. The price has always been too high. In her family, experience has taught her that being loved will cost her *self*, the most vital thing any of us has.

"I've already given too much. I can't give any more," she weeps. "Not to you. Not to anyone. Not ever!" *So this is what her basketball game means to her. I have become close enough to begin to matter, and it frightens her. She is running from it as hard as she knows how.*

"Lavonne, you don't have to give up yourself to be close to another person. We *can* be friends, and you don't have to sacrifice basketball or anything else you value. I wouldn't want you to. But I won't always understand, so you'll have to help me. I can only promise I will always try to listen." From that time on, our work together deepens. Certainly it isn't always smooth, but we understand each other better, and Lavonne has begun to trust me. In a sense, we *did* walk through a wall made of fear and pain and hurt. It barred the way between us until now.

Rene Spritz studied infants in British foundling homes after World War II. Many of their parents had been killed in air raids, and the children were kept sterile, well-nourished, and free from disease, but they had no special person with whom to bond. These infants "failed to thrive," and eventually they died. Spitz called the condition "marasmus." His findings jolted the world of psychiatry. Human beings *must* relate to each other or they die. Equally powerful, we know, is our need to individuate, to become unique independent selves. Early in development, these two drives oppose each other. They seem to conflict, to be mutually exclusive. As we mature, however, the opposing forces reveal themselves, paradoxically, as harmonious. If we are fortunate enough to resolve the oedipal conflict, as I will eventually learn, we will finally experience those seemingly contradictory forces as cooperative, increasingly inclusive, and eventually as harmonious. Lavonne *can*, for example, play basketball *and* have therapy. She just has to schedule her events. Ultimately, having done their job, the drives neutralize each other and unite in a whole and solid personality. Becoming that mature self, free of inner conflict and comfortable in relationships, is the goal of Western psychology.

CHAPTER 3:

Portrait of a Sociopath:
Up Close and Explosive

As I had, by now, long noticed, you can't keep look-ing deeply into others without discriminating them from each other and from yourself. By the time I graduate from Simmons, I am all too familiar with my own poor self-esteem. Eva Golden has nothing on me, and I know my ambivalence about relationships resembles La-vonne Dupuis'. Neither of us is as extreme as her parents, but she and I share a similar psychological structure.

Immersion in resolving interpersonal and intra-psychic conflicts teaches me that self-deprecation and am-bivalence in relationship are always found together, as if magnetically connected. You can't fix one without address-ing the other. I could live with middling self-esteem, but I did want a good relationship. Marrying someone I love wholeheartedly and raising a family has always been my major goal.

Several young men pursued me in years past, but in my heart familiarity bred contempt, while absence made it grow the fonder. I barely tolerate interested men, while developing crushes on the unattainable ones: in high school, the football hero already engaged to the head cheer-leader; in college, a friend and rising young star in the history department with decidedly platonic feelings toward me. My would-be suitors are perfectly acceptable. Many are, point for point, as desirable as the men I long for. Why do I spurn them? Even in high school, when my knowledge of psychology is limited to rats in mazes, I begin to wonder what is wrong with *me*, because there is nothing wrong with them.

Though I clearly recognize my stance toward men as a problem, I haven't gotten around to working on it, when suddenly I am in love and experiencing that ineffable and awesome state myself. I meet Jacov at Harvard Summer School, where I am taking two English courses in the summer of 1952 chiefly to enjoy Boston with my favorite cousin, Hugh. He had spent the previous summer at Harvard, getting some coursework that he needed to graduate. He's had such a great time that he has talked me into coming with him on this occasion.

Jacov Rubin is an Israeli, a *sabra*, whose parents emigrated from Russia. He has served as a commando in the *Palmach*—the striking arm of the Israeli Army—has been wounded, and carries a steel plate under the skin of his left temple from a nearly fatal wound. He is exuberant and charismatic with clear green eyes and the build of a Russian bear. He plays guitar and sings and dances the *hora*. He is the most exciting man I have ever met, *and*, for the first time in my life, the man I love, loves me. We spend a wonderful summer together, then he returns to the University of California at Davis, where he is studying veterinary medicine, and I enter Duke University as a freshman. We write to each other during the school year, and the following summer, I go to summer school at the University of California at Berkeley so we can spend three months together.

My mother insists on going with me because she is alarmed that I am interested in someone so extrinsic to her world. She will take accreditation courses for her teaching certificate, and I will take two more classes in English literature. We live in separate dormitories and rarely see each other. When I introduce her to Jacov, she is even more confounded by my interest in this enigmatic man who appears to her as from outer space. But Jacov and I are ecstatic, and we plan a trip to Israel for the following summer so that I can see his country and meet his parents.

As many young women do in those days, I arrange a student tour abroad between my sophomore and junior years of college. My mother did this herself and thought it the singularly most important educational experience of her life, so she can hardly refuse my trip, and, of course, my father never refuses me anything. For two months, I travel in Europe with my student group, but I stay on for an extra month, with parental blessings, to return to a few places I have most enjoyed, like Rome and Florence. During this month, I have already arranged to spend at least a week in Israel. I have worked all year to pay for this leg of my journey, so I will not have to involve my parents in any way. They would only disapprove and worry, and I can't ask them to fund an enterprise of which they so hardily disapprove. When I arrive in Tel Aviv, however, I find that Jacov's parents have not only welcomed him home but have *insisted* that he return, as they have heard he is interested in a *shiksa*, translated from the Yiddish as an "abomination." They have convinced him that he cannot marry me. It is a matter of his duty to his country. I am devastated, and while I am officially in the Scottish Highlands, I am actually seeing Israel through my tears.

The next time I fall in love is ten years later. This time it is with Kate's Irish Catholic father, who does marry me, even though I am not Catholic or any other religion for that matter, having unceremoniously rejected Christianity, when meeting Jacov showed me the wholly unchristlike absurdity of Christian exclusivity.

Dan is very different from Jacov, though he is also very intelligent and highly educated, a product of Boston Latin School and Georgetown University. He is also passionate. With a legal mind and a deep love of the law, he has supported himself as a policeman, like his father before him, while he finished most of his law school classes at night. Dan is a good policeman and has been promoted to plainclothes investigator in the District Attorney's office. We plan that he will finish his law degree so that he can fulfill *his* personal dream, leaving me free to work part-time to fulfill my own.

Dan and I are both overjoyed when we learn I am pregnant in the second month of our marriage. At least Dan *seems* to be overjoyed. But five months into my pregnancy he calls me one day to say he has quit his job. He will go to law school full-time. I don't understand; we need the money to augment my private practice income. There is something strange in his voice that I cannot read and that I later identify as fear and anger. Dan comes home late that night, very drunk.

He drinks the next morning. He will not talk to me. He does not return to night school and becomes so depressed that he can't move off the couch in our living room. He drinks almost nonstop and refuses help of any kind. Though he has always expressed immense respect for AA, which kept his father sober for a lifetime, he refuses to go to meetings himself. Dan has really lost it. And I have lost Dan.

What had been *our* plan of his practicing law becomes *my* plan. In his depression, he experiences me and my support of law school as forced on him, an unwelcome demand. While full of venom toward me, he also seems glued to my side. Stationed on the living-room couch, he occupies the center of our small house, its three first-floor rooms connected by large archways.

I really never learn what has precipitated Dan's sudden and deep depression. I guess it is my pregnancy, which is just beginning to show, and I assume that, in anticipation of sharing our very close relationship with a child, he feels threatened by some terrible loss. Whatever it is, he can't say, but his former love and adoration for me has radically changed. He can't admit this either, and perhaps he doesn't know it consciously, but his behavior clearly expresses that he now views me as the enemy. How can this be? He was so loving. Where have those feelings gone?

In the midst of this agony, four months pass, I go into labor—which is thankfully unremarkable—and Kate is born. Her delivery, does not resolve anything between her father and myself, but, despite the anguish surrounding it, it is an epiphany for me. For the first hour after her birth, I lie on a hospital trolley waiting for a room. A prescient nurse has positioned me just outside the nursery so that I can see my daughter in her bassinet on the other side of the glass partition. This tiny being is a *girl*, and her perfection is immediately as obvious as it is impeccable. As those countless, nameless people had looked at Rosanna, I look at Kate, mesmerized. Her face, particularly her mouth, is entirely plastic. Already, in sequences of seconds, she registers dozens of expressions, a universe of feeling, from bliss to demonic rage, from surprise to desolation, and back to rapture again. What an incredible creature. The world in a microcosm, and once I have a room and can hold her and look more closely, I see that the hair follicles are positioned on her brow to become eyebrows exactly duplicating her father's, whose brows, eyes, and his own very expressive mouth, deeply etched in my mind, are dearly loved despite the catastrophe that our relationship has become.

Once again, I fall in love. This time with Kate. I think this must be the experience of most new parents and nature's way of ensuring children's protection and nourishment. Long before the gods were male, I like to think, some primal goddess held life and death in her quickening hands, and knowing full-well how to protect her own, she cast this simple, awesome, immutable spell on humankind, the bond of motherly love.

Overwhelmingly powerful, this experience burns out the last remnants of my damaged self-esteem. The moment I fall in love with Kate, all my sins resolve. How can the author of such perfection have a fatal flaw? The idea is unthinkable. Edith Jacobson was right, along with those other wise men and women of all ages and traditions who taught that love is the balm for all ills. This no longer sounds trite to me. It is, after all, my first experience of deep and sudden conflict resolution.

Back at home and somehow always profoundly contented during my time with Kate, months pass with no change in Dan. I realize more about the adoration in which he held me and come to see his "love" as the infantile version: idealization/devaluation, not integrated, mature love. I know from my work that idealization alternates with devaluation and is a "black and white" affair. This is the bond young children have with their parents before they integrate their need for attachment with independence and move on to resolve their oedipal conflicts. As yet unmodified by these childhood tasks, Dan's feelings for me can only rise and fall between extremes. Idealization is the way in which Lavonne's parents loved her and the reason she feared they might destroy her separate self. More mature than they or than Dan, Lavonne can undertake the fairly refined task of integrating her opposing sets of feelings. Whereas her parents and Dan, far less evolved, are restricted to infantile and contradictory emotions, unmodified and thus intense. I begin to understand that Dan suffers from a severe character flaw. Why have I not recognized this before? How did I miss in him what I can see in others?

Undifferentiated as he is, Dan's self-image and his image of me have burst into shards at the same moment.

Is my pregnancy the trigger? Maybe it is something else. But, whatever it is, suddenly intimacy and I have become a threat to his survival.

Once before, and only once, I had glimpsed these dark depths in Dan. They appear when I get a haircut he doesn't like, a *haircut*, mind you. This particular style is too short. It doesn't suit me. I don't like it either, but that's life. Not for Dan, it isn't. He is angry with me, as though I have purposely ruined my looks to offend him. For two days, he won't speak. No matter how I try to reason, he only says my hair is too short for the "mother of his child."

I don't like the feel of this, but I try not to look too closely. I don't want to see what his behavior implies. As much as I try to cover my eye of knowledge, that eye never sleeps, and its truth won't deviate, no matter how hard I push it away. Deep within, Dan doesn't see me as a person in my own right, but rather as an extension of himself. I am his mirror. I reflect him, and my function is to make him feel *good*, not *bad* as I have done. This is very primitive, indeed. It is the stuff of raw narcissism. Dan doesn't comprehend the severity of his feelings and, even though I have glimpsed the threat, I deny it and proceed with our plans to marry and to have a child. Some might say it was my karma. All I can say is that—excluding my very gratifying relationship with Kate--this is the most devastating period in my life. And I cannot deny the knowledge that it is my responsibility for refusing to heed that warning, but I have to live with this, too.

From the time of his breakdown until Kate is eight months old, we remain together. I do everything I can think of to rescue Dan from his very destructive feelings, to re-engage him in a relationship with me, to restructure a plan for life as a family. Nothing works. He lies on the couch watching TV, totally paralyzed by his massive depression, made worse by almost constant drinking. Sporadically, he makes a little money driving a cab, but most of the time he drinks, he sleeps, and he is always totally closed to me.

Though he never opens up, once he tells me a dream that is very powerful for him and that reveals a great deal about the functioning of his psyche. The dream is about me. In it, I have died and Dan is heartbroken. I lie in an open casket in the back of a hearse. Reluctantly, he looks inside. To his great relief, he sees it is his mother, not me, in the coffin. So I am not dead after all. *Somebody* has died, but it isn't me. Just then his mother opens her eyes and begins to sit up. *She* isn't dead, either! Fearful that if she were not the victim, then it truly must be *me*, he tries to push her back into the coffin. Then he wakes up from the dream (which, of course, he is living out in his waking life).

The truth is that I really *have* died to Dan, and unconsciously I *am* his mother. Having become a mother, I become *his* mother, and he has to reject me as he has rejected her. Deeply ambivalent about our relationship, Dan can neither be in it nor leave it. Isolated in a drunken stupor, he remains glued to me, always in my face, refusing to move off that couch in the center of our house. Of course, he doesn't want it to be this way, no one ever does, but it *is* this way, and he can't change one jot of it.

At this point I fully register the disaster. Dan is a

very primitive type of narcissistic personality called a sociopath. A clever phrase from my training days at the BI comes back to me. With all of us struggling to differentiate pathologies, one bright resident says, "Look at it this way: A psychopath is a schizophrenic on wheels and a sociopath is a psychopath with flat tires." Dan is the latter, but in a fit of rage his tires don't look so flat. Aside from my clients, toward whom I am able to be appropriately objective, I have never seen such psychopathology up close, have never been so subjectively devastated by it, and, perhaps in some deep way, have never until now fully believed in the existence of such raw insanity.

Dan hardly comprehends what a mess he is, but I am fully aware of it and in acute pain. I can neither eat nor sleep. I am so depressed myself that I feel as though I am talking to my clients from under four feet of water. I have to read their charts before I see them so I can remember what we are working on. It is pathetic, but it is also intolerable, and I can't go on this way—not as a therapist, not as a person, and certainly not as a mother.

Since Dan can't leave me, I will have to leave him. I will have to go far away, because I know he can't leave me alone if I am within reach. In one week's time, on August 1st, I am scheduled to go with Kate to North Carolina for a month's vacation. Again, I urge Dan to go to therapy or at least to AA. I remind him that I am going to visit my family. I have to think about what to do. Living like this is not working for either of us.

Dan becomes furious. He throws furniture around the room. He does not hit me with it, which he could have done, but his reaction to the idea that I might leave him forces me to change my plans. Because Kate is totally vulnerable and I am her protector, I am rendered nearly as helpless as she is, so I am afraid to be alone with him for the week. I call my parents. They board the next plane for Boston. My poor blind father will defend me with his life if necessary. He shakes his cane at Dan and tells him not to interfere. This is not the way to handle Dan. I can see the knuckles of his clenched fists go white, but he won't hit a blind man—at least, not yet.

To this point Dan has only erupted verbally, punched holes in walls, overturned furniture, and once held a menacing fist out toward Kate. I fear he may well become violent toward me when I try to go. His rage is molten. In fact, since my parents have arrived on the heels of my telling him we may have to separate, he threatens, darkly, that I am not to leave the state with his child. He can get an injunction against me so I can't take her to North Carolina. Though I would not have thought such a thing possible, I know nothing about the law, and this threat terrifies me further.

It is now the last week of July. My parents and I decide I should leave with Kate immediately. I call my clients and cancel appointments for the rest of the week. I pack a few things in a paper bag: Kate's favorite blanket and stuffed animal, some of the toys she likes in her bath, and two or three all-purpose baby outfits. I take Kate quietly out of the house. We drive to a friend's home where I park my car. We take a cab from there to the airport. As we wait for our plane, Kate waves happily to every man she sees, calling "Dada," one of her first words.

When my sister meets us at the Raleigh/Durham airport, she says I look like I have just escaped from Auschwitz. Though that comparison is much too extreme, I *am* skin and bones and shell-shocked. Little Sarah Merriman, the fourth of my sister's five children and the cousin closest in age to Kate, comes with her mother to meet us. She hugs a small rag doll. Sarah, then two years old, sensing that Kate and I need help and that she and her mother are here to give it, leans over to her baby cousin and, very maternally, gives her the little doll. "It's just about your size," she coos. "You can call her 'Little.' That's a nice name." What a relief it is to be back in a world of sanity. My parents join us the next day. They have remained behind, on guard, until Kate and I reach safety.

PART II:

HELPING OTHERS HELPS ME

CHAPTER 4:

Beginning Again

Kate and I make it to North Carolina, and that is the critcal thing, but my life is a wreck. I take that vacation month of August to decide, but I already know I will have to leave Boston and start over. I like Boston and will miss it, but it isn't safe for us now. I'll have to go back briefly to sell the house I bought, pack it up, say good-bye to some people in person, and move, officially, to Raleigh.

My parents left Gastonia when my mother retired from teaching. They moved to Raleigh to be near my sister and her family. Dan and I went to Gastonia to help with that move. At the time, I could not have imagined that I would ever be moving to Raleigh myself. I tell Dan of that final decision by phone. He can't keep the house and doesn't want it. He cries a little but says less. I call a real-estate broker in Boston, put the house on the market, and turn to the painful and difficult task of contacting my clients. I speak with each of them to inform them that a family crisis has made it necessary for me to move to Raleigh. We do whatever sort of termination is possible by long-distance phone. I arrange with them and with colleagues for their transfer to suitable therapists.

In early September when the house sells, I leave Kate with her grandparents for the few days it takes to finish my business in Boston. Lois, my best friend from Columbia, helps me pack a truck, which, with car in tow, I will drive to Raleigh. "Well," she says, quite satisfied as we lock the truck door outside the house I no longer own, "we got it all in. No one should own more than they can carry, at least no more than they can carry in a ten-foot van."

I feel close to a number of friends in Boston and will miss them sorely, but I can't take the time at this point to see each of them and say good-bye. Now I will have to face my grief squarely and try to start another life. I dread both, but at least this time I have Kate.

Once more I look for a job. This time I have a degree and even more experience. Though it is now irrelevant, I can even type. What *is* relevant is that I am unknown in my new professional community. The director of Psychiatric Outpatient Services at Wake County Hospital, knowing only that I am relocating for family reasons, takes one look at my résumé, two looks at me, and says, "Take some time off. Soak in a warm tub. Eat bonbons. Be good to yourself. When you feel better, come back and see me." He has a point, I know, but hot baths and bonbons don't appeal to me. I keep looking for work.

Tim Underwood and Connors Putnam hire me for a part-time slot at the Child Psychiatry Outpatient Unit at Dorothea Dix Hospital. Dix is a very large state mental institution built on lavish grounds. It has lots of trees and flowers on acres of gently rolling grassy lawns, with many low brick buildings scattered randomly about the landscape. No skyscrapers or land shortage here. There is even a farm and a dairy on these grounds. It reminds me a little of McLean Hospital in Belmont, and it looks like a good place to begin again.

Dix is exclusively an inpatient facility, except for the small child psychiatry training program that Tim and Connors designed and direct. They are very innovative and energetic, intelligent and caring. Their program is excellent, and they have put together a talented staff. I am grateful to be a member of it and very happy with my part-time job. With the exception of Kate, of course, work has become the critical aspect of my life for many reasons—chiefly, because I love it, as I can no longer deny, and also because I now clearly see that it immerses me in learning the deep inner reality that has become the central, long-term interest of my life. I look at myself and at my clients, knowing we are all here through no design of our own. But that we have been given a chance to learn important, irrevocable truths about life and its larger purpose. I want to know the answers to all these hard questions. With ever increasing clarity, I see that we all must pass through the same psychological growth sequence if we are to evolve fully. We will all come to this work in unique ways, with our own specific set of issues, but the tasks we will solve are always the same. The specific design of this emotional progression is what I am clarifying for myself as I work with clients at their various sticking points. In seeing and aiding a client to unravel his Gordian Knot, I deepen my knowledge of that task, and, so, of the psychic obstacles and their potential solutions that we all encounter. This growth work is universally necessary. It has a crucial point. It leads somewhere vital. Exactly *where*, I don't know yet, but I am committed to finding out, and, in the meantime, life goes on.

Kate and I live with my parents for nine months. This works out very well for me, for Kate, and for my father, but my mother has trouble with it. She likes having us share the apartment, but, at the same time, she feels it places a demand on her for babysitting, even though my father plays with Kate all morning and I am there in the afternoons. Somehow our presence "curtails" her freedom.

I am close to my mother and understand her very well. The problems she feels in her life, though largely of her own making, nevertheless cause her stress. She feels the same sense of entrapment with my father as she does with Kate and me. Although he is quite self-sufficient, my mother doesn't like her own sense that he needs her constantly. She does like to talk to me about it. "You have a gift for understanding people," she says, "no wonder you enjoy your work." But *talk* is as far as she can take her problems. She can't act on solutions. For example, she never accepts the offer I have extended for years that she allow me to arrange a training program for my father at the world-renowned Perkins School for the Blind in Boston. Perkins offers many programs. One I thought especially suitable for my father was a weeklong course in independent-living skills, such as using canes for walking safely, crossing streets, and orienting oneself directionally by sound and the warmth of the sun. With training, many severely handicapped people like Louise Hicks live alone success-fully. This course would be a perfect primer for my father, who loves being both outdoors and independent. He is fully ready to sign on, but with a solution in sight, my mother backs off and finds excuses.

She has a great store of information, which allows her to understand rather deeply quite a lot about life and people. She understands a great deal more than my father does about abstract subjects like emotions. However, she has no insight whatsoever into her own dysfunctional be-havior, and, no matter how often the same conflict appears, she neither recognizes it nor wishes to do so. Instead, she lives out her claustrophobic feelings with my father for the greater part of their married lives, and now she repeats this with Kate and myself. In short, she loves having us around, but she hates that she *has* to have us here. This feeling of obligation about doing the "right" thing, even when there is nothing to *do*, is her lifelong plague. It was deeply imbed-ded in her psyche long before her own beloved father, on his deathbed, and with all the family in attendance, singled her out from his eight children, took her hand, and said with tears in his eyes, "Oh, it's my darling Catherine who has never caused me a moment's trouble from the day she was born." So my mother always has to do the right thing mentally, if not physically. I wouldn't be surprised to learn that during the period when Kate and I lived with them, my mother *felt* exhausted from the childcare she did not do.

Nevertheless when Kate is about sixteen months old, Mother asks that we move into our own apartment. I am a bit shocked that she would ask this, knowing how much she loves Kate and thinking surely she must understand that such a move will not be good for her development, but I do not push my case; i.e., to afford this, I will have to work full-time, and I feel Kate is much too young for another disruption with a nanny at home instead of me. Were she older, I, too, would prefer an apartment of our own, but under the circumstances I feel strongly about staying put and "making do." However, neurotic or not, it is my mother's prerogative to design her life as she wishes. My parents have been very gracious to house us for as long as they have. Though my father wants to continue the current arrangement, I accede to my mother's wishes. Nothing else seems fair.

Fortunately, I can arrange full-time work at Dix, and I find a wonderful apartment in Cameron Village, a section of Raleigh near my work with townhouse apartments on large tracts of land. The apartment I choose has its own "natural" yard space, ceded to it by logic rather than by physical boundaries. This means there are no streets between our unit and several dozen others, so Kate can play outside with safety. When she is old enough to enjoy a swing set, for example, there is a place to put it in "our" side yard where it will not be in anyone's way.

Because the conventional wisdom of the day and my own knowledge of daycare in the area tells me she is too young to be in that more impersonal situation, I find and hire a full-time nanny to be with Kate during my absence. This is how Lovey Mae Williams enters our lives. She begins her job weeks before we move so Kate can get to know her in familiar surroundings. Lovey is aptly named. She is a warm, wonderful, middle-aged woman who is always cheerful, smiling, laughing, and, most of all, deeply kind. Even so, after our move, on the first few mornings when I leave her alone with Lovey, Kate is very upset and so, of course, am I. I am also angry because I know how unnecessary this additional stress is for her, especially, but for me as well. Kate's having to suffer for my mother's neurosis is simply absurd. But soon Kate learns to love and trust Lovey, and my leave-takings are only mildly sad. Our situation is further improved by a new addition to our family.

That summer my sister's dog has puppies, and Sarah insists that we take one. I am reluctant because I won't be at home to train it, but one afternoon she brings the puppy to visit. As soon as Kate sees that tiny, curly-haired, aerial-tailed little handful of dog waddling up our walkway behind her aunt, she falls in love with him, and that is that. Of course, we have to keep him. From a story I have just read to Kate about a little boy who lost his father's hammer while helping to build a dog house, Kate chooses to name her dog Hammer. It is an unusual name for a dog, but it works. Our next-door neighbors think he is so adorable that they order one, too. They name Hammer's brother Sickle for obvious, but not political, reasons.

At first smaller and weaker than Kate, Hammer rapidly grows to be her physical size and more than her physical equal. He is a lively, eager, but gentle playmate and one of the smartest dogs I've ever known. Very soon, he recognizes that he is more responsible than Kate, and he assumes his place as her protector and guardian. From then on when I come home from work, I can immediately locate

Kate. If she is visiting a neighbor or playing with a friend, Hammer lies outside the door of that particular house in his Sphinx pose, guarding the door and waiting for Kate to reemerge. Hammer is an altogether satisfactory pet, and for all his wavy black hair, he doesn't even shed. Both Kate and I adore him.

Not surprisingly, once we are settled at Cameron Village, without skipping a beat, my mother collects Kate every day after her nap. She takes her over to the apartment where we all used to live so that Kate and Pop, as his grandchildren call my father, can play, as usual, while she makes dinner for us all. Soon she looks back with fondness on the "good old days" when she saw even more of Kate. It isn't long before she and my father also move to Cameron Village, so Kate can walk to their apartment any time she wishes. Essentially, my parents now live in our backyard.

What strange creatures we humans are. Increasingly, many adults, in addition to my mother, are looking to me like little children, walking around in full-sized bodies, creating all kinds of imaginary monsters and emotional havoc for themselves when life could be, and should be, a lot simpler than we so often make it. The challenges of the outside world are quite enough to consume our creative energies. No one need burden themselves with "fictitious" problems.

More blind than my father in her way, my mother never sees the need to change; nor, unfortunately, does Dan. He doesn't call or write or try to mend himself or the rift between us. Though our relationship was so ugly in the end, I deeply love the man he was before that severe depression broke him, and I grieve the loss of what might have been. Somewhere in my heart, that love remains, always in suspended animation, and Dan remains potentially dearly beloved, though never actually so again. His vulnerability costs him, as it does me, untold anguish, but I have to get on with life. Having Kate demands it and makes it easier, too.

In addition, as it turns out, I find my job at Dix both stimulating and challenging. I see clients but am also responsible for training social workers from various schools in the area who do their practica at Dix. This is new for me and adds another interesting dimension to my work.

Also, in an effort to increase the awareness of educators and legislators in the capitol city, we design a day-care study in the area and make a movie of ten or so different child-care situations. We present this movie at a regional psychiatric conference.

At the BI, we used a Freudian-based treatment philosophy, whereas at Dix, we and the field in general, have become deeply interested in developmental theory. With Kate's evolution a daily part of my life, I am naturally drawn to this study and soon "meld" it to the BI's dynamic model. This proves a powerful combination for teaching, training, and therapy. It also focuses my interest on the Swiss psychologist Jean Piaget, who is the most precise observer and writer on the subject of psychological development in the field. Piaget applied his theory strictly to cognitive development, though he said his carefully constructed theoretical framework would correlate equally well with the evolution of affects if applied to them. I begin a personal project of doing just that.

Piagetian Stage Progression

Stage & Age	Period / Relation	Developmental Level	Personality / Phase
Stage I, 0–1 Months	Sensorimotor Period — Sublogical Relations; Intrapersonal, concrete issues in immidiate space (unconscious)	Autism / Psychosis	
Stage II, 1–4 Months		Narcissism	Passive Narcissistic Character
Stage III, 4–8 Months		Narcissism	Active Narcissistic Character or Borderline Personality
Stage IV, 8–12 Months		Symbiosis	Passive Symbiotic Personality or Primitive Neurotic Personality
Stage V, 12–18 Months		Symbiosis	Active Symbiotic Personality or Symbiotic Neurotic
Stage VI, 18–24 Months	Representational Period (preoperational + concrete operational subperiods) — Logical Relations; Interpersonal, interactional issues in enviormental space (conscious)	Impulsive Character Organization + Development	Formative Compliant or "Oral" Personality
Stage VII, Preconceptual, 2–4 Years		Impulsive Character	Passive Ego-centric Oppositional or "Anal" Personality
Stage VIII, Simple intuitions 4–5+ Years and Articulated intuitions 5+7 Years (Stages IA and B)		Impulsive Character	Active Ego-centric or "Phallic" Personality — Oedipal Conflictual Phase
Stage IX, Initial Concrete Operational Period, 7–9 Years (Stage IIA)		Neurosis	Neurotic or "Genital" Personality — Oedipal Resolution Phase
Stage X, Mature Concrete Operational Subperiod, 9–11 Years (Stage IIB)		Neurosis	Pure Neurotic State or "Oedipal" Personality — Oedipal Integration Phase
Stage XI, Formal Operational Period Begins, 10–15 Years (Stages IIIA & B)	Formal Operational Period — Metapersonal, philosophical issues in universal space; abstract consciousness with hypothetical & deductive reasoning	Autonomy	Mature or "Autonomus" Personality Consolidation Phase

CHAPTER 5:

Piaget's Science of Psychology

Piaget takes his core ideas about the development of intelligence in children from Darwinian biology. He refuses to call his work psychology because he thinks the evolution of intelligence in human beings is most like the adaptation of physical organisms to their environment. He refers to himself as a genetic epistemologist and bases his theory on the premise that two forces drive development. One is the organism's need to assimilate its environment, as in eating. The other is its need to accommodate to its habitat, altering itself to harmonize more comfortably and safely with its surroundings. An example of this accommodation is the behavior of molluscs found in Eurasian marshes which actively alter their long and narrow shape to become "shortened and globular" when found along the windy, agitated shores of the regions' lakes. Piaget studied these molluscs and published papers on them when he was a high school student. (1)

Self-definition demands distinction between self and other. Improving inner organization and increasing environmental awareness improves communication and creates a keener sense of self and other. This, in turn, produces a new relationship between the evolved entities, setting up a new cycle which in turn causes the organism to pick up fresh cues from outside, and to respond by reorganizing again. By organizing and reorganizing in this way, the organism evolves. Some twenty-five years later, an important theorist named Margaret Mahler espouses ideas quite close to Piaget's. She says children grow emotionally as a function of contrasting wishes to join with their caregiver on the one hand and to separate on the other. She also notes the push/pull along the developmental continuum increasing children's knowledge of self and simultaneously of other, enhancing their capacity for closeness and intimacy. Essentially both Piaget and Mahler claim that to exist is to relate, and that relationship is the motor of development.

Virtually all theorists postulate a set of dual psychic principles and a relationship between them that impels psychic growth. For Freud, it is the relationship between the libidinal and the aggressive drives. For Object Relations theorists, like Mahler, it is the urge to separate in concert with the urge to bond in the early mother/child dyad that becomes imprinted in the child's psyche. Therefore, at the level of psychic organization, Piaget's assimilation and accommodation process, Freud's drive conflict, and Mahler's dual urges point to the same thing. Conflicting or complementary, primary needs for closeness as well as for individuality activate the psyche and propel development forward.

I find additional help with Piaget's developmental system in his work with adolescents. *Logic and Psychology* is a small book based on three lectures Piaget gave at the University of Manchester in 1952. Dr. Wolfe Mays, an eminent philosopher from Manchester Metropolitan University in Britain, translates and introduces the volume, pairing formal logic with Piaget's stages. Stage I is a stage of fusion. (2) Here the innate psychic forces are in an undifferentiated mass of relationship with each other. This is the psychotic's core design. Since no self exists in this boundless state, for its first few weeks of life, infants cannot know if sights or sounds come from inside or outside. Instead, they live in a hallucinatory state. Reflexive behavior operates to "train" infants to find the breast and the nipple, to suck for nourishment and for the pleasure of satisfying their strong innate sucking reflex.

Stage II's design is an all-or-nothing relationship of the urges with each other. This stage lasts for about four months while the urges achieve a beginning differentiation by eclipsing each other, one fully suppressed to expose the other and vice versa. At this point, infants do have a boundary, a very rigid one, which forms what Piaget calls acquired associations or "habit chains." The most common example of a habit chain is systematic thumb sucking, a learned behavior requiring a rather complex coordination of hand, mouth, and vision. In the adult who exhibits Stage II as his core design, we see a Narcissistic Personality. Heinz Kohut studied these self-centered, "mirroring," or "idealizing" individuals whose focus on self renders them unable to love or to empathize. (3)

At Stage III the two better-differentiated urges relate to each other in an either/or mode, one urge up and active (idealized), while the other is down and inactive (devalued). Stage II is rigid, while Stage III has a volatile nature, frequently alternating between modes. Piaget calls this new behavior "Secondary Circular Reactions" or "Procedures Destined to Make Interesting Sights Last." Here infants prolong or repeat an effect that happens by chance and begin to differentiate between means and ends, but only because they focus on the results of their actions and want to reproduce them. Piaget describes his daughter, Lucienne, kicking her legs while lying in her bassinet and noticing that a doll hanging from the hood swings. She seeks to repeat this play and eventually succeeds in making the connection between her kicking and the result she wants. Because the child has not understood the mechanism of the action, Piaget says this is not yet truly "intelligent" behavior. In adults with developmental delay, this either/or behavior lies at the core of the borderline personality, who switches back and forth between an outrageously angry persona and an extremely passive or needy one. Like their infantile counterparts, older persons stuck at this stage neither control nor understand what activates their mood swings.

At Stage IV, the relationship between the urges is of twinship or of both/and. Here relationship urges coexist as nearly separate entities, though to retain validity, they must remain in accord with each other. This accord foreshadows the formation of a psychic overview that will later become the observing ego or witness consciousness, the "director of the psyche" and the critical feature in any mature personality. At Stage IV, the two urges cannot express themselves independently as they will do at V. Stage IV is the hallmark of ambivalence, the proverbial donkey starving between two bales of hay. Piaget calls it "The coordination of the Secondary Schemata (the habit chains from Stage II) and Their Application to New Situations." (4) It is at Stage IV that Piaget identifies the first intelligent behavior as children set out to perform a desired action (their ends), understanding the mechanism for accomplishing it (their means). Between eight and twelve months, infants learn to find a person's glasses even if the glasses are hidden behind a pillow. Out of sight is no longer out of mind. The unseen object has not "reentered the void" as it seemed to do at previous stages. These children can hold the goal in mind while they search their repertoire of means to accomplish it. However, even though they watch while the glasses are hidden behind a *second* pillow, they remain "egocentrically" tied to their first successful experience and invest this with more reality than the glasses. Therefore, they will go only to the first pillow, where they retrieved the prize that first time, and will not look behind the second, even though they *saw* the glasses placed there.

At Stage V, children's mental capacities have increased sufficiently to encompass what Mays calls the "if… then" or implicative stage of rapid shuttling. Now, action—entirely dependent upon memory after the fact of its occurrence—is retained and children begin to take ownership of their actions. They are no longer behaviorally merged with their parents or with the solipsistic, magical power they gave their connection to objects previously. Margaret Mahler's 2nd Practicing Subphase Proper (the child's love affair with the world) occurs here also.

It is children's experiments at Stage IV that eventually lead them from egocentricity to the more objective science of Stage V's cause and effect. At V, they believe more fully in the "conservation" of objects and in the basic laws of motion and gravity. Piaget's clear examples and interesting details of these infantile experiments make them worth a moment's notice. In the preceding data, especially during the second half of the first plateau, we have seen the ability to internalize thought developing slowly, and though it does not emerge as a solid accomplishment until the second plateau, these experiments also merit attention because they describe the critical turning point in the profoundly significant process of internalizing abstract ideas.

Piaget's ten-month-old son Laurent is playing with a cake of soap. At Stage IV, Laurent is limited to the egocentric activity of letting go of the soap to see it fall. He still does not understand the role of gravity, so in his high-chair, he is letting objects go without knowing what will happen to them. Piaget comments that the child can only reproduce the "result observed fortuitously" when he picks up the object and "lets go of it," watching it fall to the floor. Laurent studies the varied results of "letting go," but soon he shows more interest in the fate of the object than in his own action. A few days later, Laurent is playing with a piece of bread. After letting it go several times—sometimes even "pushing the bread down" to insure that it will reach the floor (Stage IV behavior like the glasses behind pillow No. 1)—his attention begins to shift from his own pushing and letting the bread go to watching intently as the "body in motion" falls to the floor unaided.

By Stage V, at age one, the child's behavior changes, and the crude experiments of Stage IV become the "goal-oriented" activities of Stage V. Laurent has previously tried to move a table with revolving tiers toward himself by pulling at it and being surprised when only the tier turns and the table itself does not move closer. Now he sees a stone on the far side of a tier. He tries only once to reach the stone by pulling the whole table toward himself, then immediately he rotates the tier to bring the stone within reach. Similarly, one-year-old Jacqueline is seated on a coverlet trying to grasp her duck, which is out of reach. In the process, she accidentally moves the coverlet and notices the duck shake. She immediately understands the connection and pulls the coverlet toward her until she can reach her toy. (5)

At Stage V, children's previously static mental "snapshots" become "motion pictures" that include the movement of objects as part of the object's identity and no longer as part of the child's. Now, round objects become rollable instead of egocentrically "rolled by me." At implicative Stage V, the nonconcrete, intangible, and nonverifiable activity that depends on memory for proof is retained. This is the first internalization of an abstraction. With the inclusion of "invisible" imagery, the child can make nonegocentric inferences about causation that are valid for him. Now, so to speak, if he sees smoke, he knows there must be fire, and now he understands that his perceptions of reality have an explanation, whether he has discovered it yet or not. The infant has reached Stage VI and has become a scientist.

Since it will be instructive in differentiating the emotional stages that I took from Piaget's cognitive ones, I will devote Chapters 6 and 7 to illustrating the continuum of emotional stages which parallel Piaget's cognitive ones.

CHAPTER 6:

Case Examples of the Stages on the First Plateau

At Stage I, the self/other signature or operational paradigm is that of fusion. Here the child or older individual operating at this core level is undifferentiated. His worldview is boundariless and he is disconnected and disorganized. Unaware of an inside or an outside, this person cannot distinguish the real from the imagined. Consolidating a self, drawing that first psychological boundary between self and other, is the critical task of Stage I.

Jonathan is a twenty-four year-old catatonic schizophrenic who still lives with his parents. He is recovering from his fourth breakdown in six years. Following several weeks of rigid catatonia, he has returned to his more usual state of rather frequent hallucinations. In these, figures on television or popular songs on the radio speak to him in "coded" messages. Very often these messages concern special medicines he alone must find to cure his mother's cancer.

As I get to know him and begin to understand his way of thinking, I see that he, like a newborn, experiences life as shifting chaos, kaleidoscopic fragments. Lacking the logic of connectivity, causal relations mean nothing to him. Reality is splintered and non-sequential. Consciousness exists but floats free without internal coordinates to lend perspective and to place him relative to the world of objects. Unlike an infant, however, Jonathan can manage some familiar routines normally because he has learned to do so at superficial psychic levels. Jonathan is fortunate because medication stabilizes him and, even though his mother is ill, his parents are willing to help with his rehabilitation. They are keenly aware of the consequences of Jonathan's isolation with radio or TV.

As his therapist, I work with Jonathan and his family to establish and monitor an outpatient program that will keep him actively connected to others. Following his discharge, I meet with him in twice-a-week therapy. I notice when he seems "different," cavalier or slightly "high." This alerts me that he may not be taking his medication as prescribed, and I confront him.

"You don't seem quite yourself today. What's going on?" If I am right, and if he will admit it, we might forestall another break. Then Jonathan begins to bring his medication to the sessions and takes his pill in my presence. After several weeks of this and my futile attempts to understand why, finally, shaking and tearful, Jonathan admits that his Haldol (a very effective antipsychotic medication for him) is stamped with an *H*. This is the first initial of his best friend Harold's name. Each time he takes it, he thinks of the communion wafer, signifying the body of Christ, and each day this precipitates a disturbing struggle with the psychotic fantasy that he is cannibalizing Harold. When he is with me, the pill is just a pill, and he can take it without the least misgiving. This fantasy becomes the focus of our reality-testing work and proves invaluable as a therapeutic tool.

After four or five years, seeing me less frequently as time goes by, Jonathan is leading a more normal life devoid of hallucinations and terrifying fantasies. Surprisingly enough, though he continues to need medication, he eventually holds a steady job as a bus driver and marries a Stage II woman who loves and understands him and who helps him stay "on point."

The Stage II signature is the all-or-nothing of psychological eclipsing. Piaget says the joining and separating urges are "globally" united at this point, each appearing in the other's absence, like two sides of a coin. The formal psychiatric diagnostic term for a Stage II adult is narcissism. The name comes from Greek mythology, which recounts the story of young Narcissus, so smitten with his own beauty that he angers the Gods, who decree he spend his lifetime gazing at his reflection in a pool.

As fusion is the major feature of Stage I, so mirroring and idealizing are the twin hallmarks of Stage II. An idealizing adult sees all the world's traffic on a one-way street moving toward himself, and is preoccupied with his "grandiosity" in all respects; whereas, the mirroring adult reverses the signpost and sees activity moving in the opposite direction. Fictional examples of mirroring personalities are Casper Milquetoast and Uriah Heap—anxious to please, always fitting in with the program, presenting no personal agenda. Of course, this is mock selflessness. The mirroring narcissist "hooks his wagon to a star" and is happiest existing in the afterglow of another's life force. Even though the focus of the mirroring narcissist is on the other, that other is *his* reflecting pool and validates the adoring one, who is no less self-absorbed than his obviously vain counterpart. Grandiose entitlement and helpless isolation are Stage II's feeling modes. This condition was poignantly described by one such person, a friend and also a therapist, as living "on the outside of a window, looking in at life but never participating in it."

Stage II modes are monolithic or preambivalent— as are the feeling states at each of the first three stages. Without a beginning overview—incipient only at Stage IV—a self-centered point of view prevails. The Stage II personality is either all entitlement or all worthless reflection of that entitlement. Primitive monolithic egos do not yet allow for a mix of emotions.

Gina is a dramatic example of Stage II, at its preambivalent and monolithic height. Her story presents a painful and divisive tale. Intense like Jonathan but with her unique Stage II form, Gina is desperately caught in a deep and constant schism at her core. She feels herself literally as two selves with two wills.

An incessantly recurring dream graphically illustrates her predicament. The dream depicts one Gina chasing the other, both in small cars traveling at high speeds. The sole aim of the one is to join the other. The sole aim of the other is to elude the one. If the Gina-cars meet, they will destroy each other in a fiery crash. The resounding message is that Gina is doomed. Since she can't live a life of such division, she must heal her psychic rift. But if unity is Gina's only hope of survival, her psyche screams that such an integration means instant death.

Though she has never had a psychotic episode, Gina's situation is reminiscent of Jonathan's. Like his, her pain and suffering are major. Like his, her peace and productivity are seriously compromised. Jonathan's psychic design or emotional template is one of fragmentation; without an inner/outer boundary he is vulnerable to hallucinating, confusing the origin of thoughts and feelings. Gina has a psychic boundary, but her separate self is cleft. Her paralysis is not of psychotic proportions, and she is able to remain in college where she is, fortunately—perhaps inescapably—a philosophy major. Gina has accomplished the first critical psychological and relational task—she owns a separate self, but being strictly divided against that self, she can do little more than Jonathan to make her way in the world.

It is sometimes difficult for Gina to think in psychological terms. So, in our sessions, she talks with me about philosophy, which I then translate into psychological meaning in philosophical language for her use. She gives me new insight into Jean Paul Sartre's existentialism and into his characters from *Nausea* and *No Exit*. Gina seems the quintessence of Sartre's "inconsequential man," whose every act is a predetermined negation of every other act.

Gina is a dramatic example of a Stage II personality, but not a typical one. All are split as their stage design dictates, but most organize themselves around one or the other side of the coin and remain as mirroring or as idealizing personalities throughout their lives. However, Gina's drama reveals the configuration of the stage like an X-ray reveals the bone structure of a body and so illustrates the underlying principles and functioning of Stage II. She presents us with a good learning case.

The signature of Stage III is either/or. At this point the developmentally stuck child or adult sees the world as filled with victims and tyrants. Carolyn comes to therapy complaining of her husband. She calls herself a victim and her husband a tyrant. Eventually, she admits that she is also an alcoholic and that this causes most of her marital discord. Unable to see that her drinking "victimizes" Jim and makes her *his* tyrant, she insists that she drinks because Jim's temper frightens her. She also reveals that she is severely depressed much of the time and has made two serious suicide attempts. She describes being a perfectionist in her housekeeping, and she correctly understands this as an effort to gain some control over her life. I know her lack of control arises from her feelings still structured as "groups," which means she lacks an overview. Carolyn has no way to "see" what she feels until she puts her emotions into action. Only an observing ego will allow her to watch her thoughts and direct her activities in an intentional manner. Carolyn soon realizes that when she is not devaluing him, she idealizes Jim and looks to him for rescue. Her extreme *split* view of her husband—as well as of her universe—is typical of the Borderline Personality's either/or psychic organization. (3)

Stage IV is an exciting stage. Piaget identifies the child's fourth-stage activities as representing the "first truly intelligent behavior patterns." On each plateau, I call this fourth stage the "psychological watershed." Piaget refers to the first three stages as "preparation" and to the second three as "fruition." A great deal of preparatory work goes into a fourth-stage result, and on any plateau, Stage IV is one of high profile. Since growth takes less time during a fruition phase, people who progress to this point have better prognoses. Like a boulder, the psyche must be "pushed," as it were, uphill to Stage IV, where downward momentum helps it roll toward Stage VI completion.

Stage IV is Piaget's stage of object permanence and the developmentalists' stage of separation and stranger anxiety. Because of his new capacity to retain a mental image, the Stage IV child experiences out of sight as lost forever. Now, parental absence threatens loss and, for the same reason, the presence of an unknown person threatens parental displacement.

The emotional signature of Stage IV is both/and. Dynamically, it is the stage of twinning. The Stage IV child overcomes the notion of victims and tyrants and replaces it with bullies and the bullied. Here I recognize my mother on the continuum with her spurious sense of being "controlled." As a Stage IV personality, she also has to act in accord with her husband, but to call him her "tyrant" (an absolute ruler who governs without restriction) is too strong a term, whereas "bully" (a habitually harsh and overbearing person, especially toward a weaker one) fits her view precisely. She feels "bullied" by my father's demands that she cook his food just so, in a way she can never manage no matter how hard she tries (nor can she give up this doomed struggle to please him, though I think he could never recognize a success even if she hit on a brilliant one). My parents care for each other, even though this stubborn Stage IV struggle subtly underlies their relationship. The two modes in this stage are the dominant bully and the dominated "underdog" whom he bullies.

Kenneth is an example of a Stage V personality. He comes to therapy when a woman he has loved for five years begins dating another man. Though Jean has never made a commitment to Kenneth, he has continued to pursue her, and when she is clearly unavailable, Kenneth becomes acutely depressed. "Men aren't supposed to cry," he tells me, "but that's all I'm good for these days."

Kenneth is depressed not just because he feels deserted, but also because he feels devalued. It's one thing to suffer and grieve a loss, but it is quite another to experience that loss as a blow to one's worth. Loss doesn't dent self-esteem, but feeling rejected does. Grief doesn't make a person feel unlovable, but "unworthiness" is the very essence of depression. Kenneth, like many others, has to deal with both at once because his loss happens before he is psychologically ready to grieve. Therapy will facilitate his grief-work, but its major task will be to formulate, focus, and implement his sense of his own worth.

Kenneth has managed to fill his potential relationship void with a real or imagined girlfriend until now. To accomplish this, he befriends a schoolmate or fantasizes a girlfriend with whom he imagines being "best friends." In this way, he has escaped feeling alone before and is astonished at the depth of his despair.

Despite substantial intellectual achievements, friendships, and a successful career, Kenneth and I can identify that he is at Stage V. With all his accomplishments, his self-esteem lags far behind where it ought to be. Although consciously he longs for one, Kenneth discovers he is highly ambivalent about an intimate partner and has never allowed himself an available woman, but always chooses someone who dominates him, insisting that he accommodate her. It is the relationship pattern his mother taught him and the only kind of intimacy he knows. The two modes available to the Stage V personality are the active pursuer or the inactive pursued.

In order to change his pattern, Kenneth must understand it deeply. His particular kind of ambivalence is Stage V's if...then of implication, which allows him to behave independently and to have a life of his own without remaining in mirroring or idealizing mode (II). His core design does not require that a person become a tyrant in his life (III) or that they always agree with him (IV). He is, instead, like the infant in "practicing subphase proper," who can go his way and allow his partner to go hers. It is only when he knows hc has irreparably lost her support (and understands he can not return for emotional reinforcement), that his confidence shatters and he falls apart.

At a fifth position on the first plateau, separation still means life or death to Kenneth, showing that he has not advanced to the second plateau. A Civil War buff, when his critical relationship ends, he suffers bloody nightmares of Gettysburg, Fort Sumter, or Bull Run—battlefields littered with the dead and dying. Despite his growth and his near readiness to be whole, separation feels fatal to him. He is on the first plateau but ready to take an important step forward.

With his therapist's help, he "witnesses" himself in operation and "watches" his two conflicting selves instead of identifying with either. The therapist's role here is to "lend" him that missing observational ego, making sure he can, with this support, really see and understand his conflict, so as to internalize a strong observational ego of his own. When he has done so, he is a Stage VI personality, a "well-wrapped" one, too, since his first two layers of psychic development are packed with useful information and important skills for living a satisfying and happy life.

CHAPTER 7:

Second-Plateau Case Examples Juxtaposed with First

J onathan is our familiar example of a Stage I fusion personality. He has no psychic boundary at his core. His corresponding stage on the second plateau is Stage VI. A completion and an initiation stage, VI concludes the first plateau of sensorimotor intelligence and inaugurates the personality onto the Representational Plateau of second-level development. The progression from stage to stage, as well as the stage signature, and the relationship between the two urges, remain the same on both plateaus, but the material processed differs in each. As we saw, the first plateau treats physical objects in the external world. The second plateau deals with those same objects but now as mental representations, internalized, and thus manipulated in thought. We might summarize: First-plateau material is external, intense, and fragmented. Second-plateau material is internal, neutralized, and integrated. An ever-growing and ever-more-encompassing neural network increasingly reflects self-consciousness as the "observational ego" that first shows itself at Stage IV and begins initial operation at Stage V. This witness consciousness continues to reflect expanding neural complexity, which now handles simple abstraction as the child matures throughout the second plateau.

Clara, as a child, and Abigail, as an adult, are Stage VI personalities. Clara and Abigail know they are separate. They know they have separate psychologies and wills of their own. Unlike the fusion of Stage I, where concrete physical fragmentation prevails, Stage VI personalities—with their solid material bodies and separate psychological selves—are fused mentally and thus confuse their thoughts and wishes with those of others. They are "pleasers," somewhat dependent and unusually amenable to suggestion. I call Stage VI personalities "Compliant."

I meet Clara when she is eight years old and her parents bring her to the child guidance clinic, complaining that she "lives in her brother's shadow." Her brother, Charlie, is ten and a lively and confident boy with a number of friends in the neighborhood. Despite their efforts to encourage Clara to follow her own interests, she always chooses to play with Charlie and his friends, where her role is inevitably "the foreign terrorist." On the school playground, she is equally docile, taking the least prestigious role on any team without a murmur. Clara does well in school. She seems healthy and well adjusted except for this issue of "letting others walk over her."

Something is wrong in Clara's life, but fortunately her problem is easily fixed. After several weeks of meeting together, Clara begins to trust me, and she confides that she loves her brother. His games are fun. Besides, he is commander-in-chief of the whole neighborhood. Why shouldn't he be hers, too? She tells me she doesn't always comply. She never allows Charlie to interrupt her home-work. She likes school more than he does and thinks she may be a better reader.

"But doesn't it make you mad that you always have to be the enemy and are taken prisoner or shot in those games? Why can't you change sides? Why can't you win against Charlie sometimes?" I ask. Immediately, I see Clara's eyes light up with interest. It seems the thought has never occurred to her. I put some toy soldiers on the play table.

At first Clara sets out her soldiers five against one. She pushes the others into the background, saying, "We don't need them." The game commences, and after a few minutes of heavy combat, the small platoon is forced to retreat. Reinforcements are air-lifted from the back of the table.

Again the battle rages. This time it is a draw, but the solitary enemy soldier still stands on its own small wooden feet, undaunted if not victorious.

"That little soldier, all by itself, is very strong," I comment. "How can it keep fighting like that with so many troops against it?"

"It has an idea," Clara says, enigmatically.

"It must be a powerful idea," I say. "What is it?"

"The idea is that it doesn't have to get killed."

"That *is* a powerful idea," I reply.

This is the first of a series of sessions. Progres-sively, Clara fights back more and more vigorously. In the months that follow these self-affirming meetings, I encourage Clara to take the lead and to choose how we spend our time together. Her parents report that she isn't playing with Charlie so much now. She seems to have grown up at last. Now Clara has one or two special girlfriends and seems to prefer them and their games to Charlie's.

Clara reminds me of my eighteen-month-old daughter. She is her own person but just barely and not with enough confidence to assume full independence. Soon I work with a mother who presents an adult version of Clara. If there were an eighteen-month-old Kate in eight-year-old Clara, there is an eighteen-month-old Clara in forty-year-old Abigail Stevens. My initial insight that many adults are children in grown-up bodies is firmly crystallizing, and I begin to see the "child" in *all* my problem clients.

As I get to know Abigail, I see she is a highly competent person with a rich personality that shows in her hearty laugh. She appreciates her own accomplishments and knows she is good at almost everything she does; however, she suffers from insomnia. Sometimes she wakes in the night with a feeling of rage that frightens her. She can't get back to sleep, and she is so uncomfortable that she gets up and works. This is one reason she accomplishes so much. We agree that her insomnia is prompted by nearly conscious anger and that her anger is forcefully repressed by her workaholic behavior. Uncomfortable or not, we need to look at her negative feelings.

Abigail is the daughter of a poor but proud farm family from the Appalachian Mountains of North Carolina. One day she complains about being seen at school getting out of her father's old pickup truck with its two doors each a different shade of blue. Her father looks her straight in the eye and says, "Abigail, I get up every morning at sunrise, I put on a clean shirt and a clean pair of overalls, and I work to the very best of my ability until there's no more light left to work by. I never buy anything I can't pay for, and, to my knowledge, I've never in my life cheated or mistreated another living thing. I don't see that there's anything for either of us to be ashamed of."

Abigail never forgets the perspective these words throw on life. Nor does she forget her mother's credo that hangs on the kitchen wall. It depicts an Olympic champion, and underneath the discus thrower are the words, "Only stretching beyond your best is good enough."

Abigail has lived her life by these principles, and she's never questioned herself as to her feelings of personal satisfaction. Now she has to admit that not only is she dissatisfied but that she is moderately depressed. Abigail cries in our sessions as she has never cried before. She is tired of being "a girl scout," and finally she becomes overtly angry. She recalls many poignant scenes when, as a child, she was called upon to put out fires and staunch blood flowing from the wounds of her younger siblings because her mother was away tending her own elderly parents. Like Clara, Abigail needs to get that "powerful idea" that you don't always have to accept delivery of the negative roles and chores in life. She needs to learn that such sacrificial behavior does not work any better for the beneficiaries than it does for the benefactors. And, as with Clara, Abigail's therapy is relatively easy, though it takes a lot of painful introspection and a lot of working through her depressed and angry feelings.

I conclude that the relative ease and success rate of therapy with these second plateau personalities happens because, despite their more sophisticated internal dynamics, they have previously developed core selves. Therefore, they are not afraid to get close, to open up, and to have meaningful remedial relationships. Unlike people on the first plateau—Jonathan, Gina, Carolyn, my mother, and Kenneth—these second-plateau clients do not fear an invasion of self in connecting to others. For them, the hardest and most threatening psychological lessons were learned before they come to therapy. Such clients are advanced and "neurotic," as opposed to delayed and "dysfunctional," and, as noted above, their prognoses are comparatively positive. At these second-plateau stages, developmental work consists of constructing subtle psychological self-concepts, not gross "physiological" ones, such as the neophyte must build. Child development brings starkly to light the "child who is father to the man or woman" in all of us. Adding this developmental perspective to my original dynamic one has made a difference, and as it becomes embedded in my professional skill set, I see I am more effective at my work.

It isn't long before my own "impish" eighteen-month-old daughter advances to her next stage and becomes a two-year-old "monster." This stage is far from subtle. As with the separation-anxiety stage, one would have to be a very absent parent indeed to miss it. Here's where children blatantly assert their need to take charge. What used to be a teasing game becomes a serious battleground on which children must assert their wills, must get a rise out of their parents. They must test the thesis that they are their own persons.

Peter Blos, a renowned adolescent psychologist, called adolescence the "second separation, individuation phase." (1) By this he means that the two-year-old's rebellion presages the adolescent's in kind and quality. Suddenly, at about this time, most parents are confronted with a pint-sized "adolescent" in full revolt. Here, at Stage VII, the curtain rises on another important psychological drama, "the Terrible Twos."

No longer docile, no more tractable or distractible, these little people mean to prove they control their own destinies. The self-assertion that my daughter displays at age two is really what Clara and Abigail needed to learn in therapy. For their own differing reasons, something interrupted their acquiring this knowledge when they were chronologically two.

With each new child stage to which my daughter introduces me, I focus attention on its dynamic and recognize it more clearly in the adults I see around me. When she becomes a "terrible two," almost everywhere I look I see other "two-year-old" adults. When I turn on the television, there is Archie Bunker. He is clearly a black-and-white thinker, verbally intimidating but lovable in his way. Beneath his macho-man Stage VII façade, which doesn't allow him to be "soft" on anything and maintain his sense of manliness, he really does care for Edith and, in the end, he even cooperates with her.

His all-or-nothing thinking is always led by emotions. It has no logic. His positions and his arguments go together in composite, subjectively determined clumps, with no causal connections between them. For example, he sees people as either tough through and through, red-blooded, football-loving, beer-drinking Americans or as commie, pinko, sexual "preverts." There is no extenuation here—a terrible two in adult disguise if I'd ever seen one. However, his second-stage position on the second plateau would be very hard to confuse with Gina's on the first.

At the clinic, Colonel Ronald Royal presents us with his teenage son Bobby as a "serious behavioral problem," and with himself as a good example of a Stage VII or "Oppositional Personality." Col. Royal is "Air Force, retired." He lives with his wife, Lilly, and their son Bobby in a small retirement home near a local military base.

Bobby is seventeen and the last of three siblings, born six years after the other two. But he isn't like the other two, neither of whom has given their parents such trouble. Bobby disobeys all the rules, big and small, from keeping his reading light on after hours to taking his father's car without permission so he can drive his girlfriend to a movie. Col. Royal, being who he is, calls the police, who take Bobby into custody as he leaves the theater. But the worst scene occurs at home after the colonel and Bobby return from the station. Instead of gratitude at being released, which the colonel expects, Bobby is enraged about his arrest. He swears at his father and hits him. Col. Royal swings back, and the two of them battle physically while Mrs. Royal looks on in horror.

These two males seem locked in psychological warfare, and we have to assess carefully that neither

Bobby nor his father is likely to inflict a major injury on the other, not on purpose anyway. This is the stuff of the "neurotic" segment of psychological stages. It is fierce, but it isn't deadly.

Lilly has raised the first two children essentially alone, because her husband was absent, working or overseas at the time. She is familiar with the kind of healthy opposition that children need to express as they develop, but her husband is unreasonably short-tempered and harsh. Lilly finds herself defending Bobby. A crack appears in the ground between the two parents. Over the years it widens. Col. Royal accuses Lilly of spoiling Bobby and of opposing him. She feels judged and deserted. And Bobby, as is true when parents fail to stand united on discipline, falls into the abyss that divides them. He has no consistent rules. His mother is too easy on him, his father is too harsh, and he is confused.

As their joint therapist, I meet with the Royals and tell them that they are the key to solving this family problem. Lilly understands what I mean, but the colonel is indignant, deeply offended. True to the black-and-white thinking of an Archie Bunker, any offense is of court-martial proportions to him. He has brought *Bobby* here for therapy. He doesn't need any himself. In fact, he won't stand for this outrage. He wants to talk to the director of the clinic, "a man, who can understand the importance of discipline." I remain firm and tell him I respect his position. It is difficult, frightening, to have a son of Bobby's age who seemingly obeys no rules. Lilly agrees with me, and gradually Col. Royal begins to listen to us as we both make it clear that we are listening to him. In time, the Royals do get their act together, and *together* they make sense. With her husband's cooperation, Lilly is no longer too lax with Bobby and, knowing he can count on her support, Col. Royal doesn't have to play "bad cop." Instead, they are codisciplinarians, both teachers, no longer one commander and one saboteur. Clara and Abigail, from one developmental level, need to learn assertion. Col. Royal, from the next level, needs to soften his aggressiveness.

Stage VIII of simple and articulated intuitions is the high-profile stage that caught Freud's eye, the stage of oedipal conflict. It covers three developmental periods. First, the "phallic" phase, or the "Oedipal Conflictual Phase" proper, then the "Resolution (IX)" and "Integration (X)" phases. As Gwendolyn taught about the Goldens, we know that beginning sometime during the late anal period, children feel phallic, genital interests. Usually the male child connects these sensations to his mother and the female child to her father. They make their preferences quite obvious, as when a young nephew of mine, hearing my husband's key in the lock, literally bolts from his chair and wedges himself tightly into mine wearing a canary-feather smile. He wants to make it clear that he and I belong together and are excluding my husband.

In my own childhood, I recall preferring my father to my mother in certain ways (and her to him in others), but I know that when I grow up I will marry someone like my father, which, eventually, I do. Furthermore, as I have mentioned, I clearly remember as a college student dating many interesting and interested young men, but, though I know they are all of marriageable quality, I am unable to return their feelings. Instead, the young men who attract me are always the ones who are emotionally unavailable to me for a variety of reasons. When I fall in love with the Israeli at Harvard, I am surprised and delighted to see that he loves me, too.

But that ends badly with my heart broken and with a long and painful recovery ahead of me. It is so painful at the time that there is precious little consolation in realizing I have finally made that oedipal passage. I take no comfort in the fact that I can finally love and be loved in return. Stages VIII and IX are so extraordinarily difficult for me because, as I see in retrospect, I am not a solid VIII going into that doomed Israeli affair. The resistance I show in college to enter the stage at all proves the point, as does the fact that I "hang on" to my grief and suffer deeply for longer than usual or necessary.

Gregory Chernobov, a five-year-old, is a healthier example of Stage VIII. His mother is a "Southern lady" from Texas with beautiful blue eyes and a very big truly "Texan" personality. She, like Eva Golden, fills a room, but she graciously leaves space for others. She is married to another big personality, named Imre. Imre is a Hungarian scientist and inventor who can trace his ancestry back, not so long ago either, to royalty. Early on he finds a reason to recite to me a very long list of Hungarian Pulitzer Prize–winning composers, Nobel laureates, inventors, architects, etc., ending, essentially, with, "And on a per-capita basis, since we are, after all, a very small country, that makes the rest of the world genetic, intellectual, and cultural pigmies." Seeing my expression, he laughs good-naturedly and adds that his position is much more liberal than his mother's, "She thinks Christopher Columbus was right on the mark when he reported that the New World was populated with savages." This is Gregory's dad.

For about a year Gregory has shown a marked preference for his mother over his father. Smiling mischievously when his father is around, he inserts himself between his parents or positions himself next to his mother, like my young nephew, clearly claiming his territory. *He* is taking possession of his mother, and that is that. Both the Chernobovs are educated people. They know about Freud and Oedipus, but this behavior can dent even Hungarian pride, and, despite what they know about normal development, they are a little anxious to confirm that what they see at home *is* normal.

Especially as he is contending with these two, we clinicians think Gregory is doing just fine. He has a little trouble achieving "laureate" standards in school, and he is jealous of his father and possessive of his mother, but this is age-appropriate. It is a normal oedipal conflict. Our clinical consensus is that Gregory will resolve it all by himself. However, these big personalities to whom he was born give us pause. There is some marital discord, too. As with the Royals, we think a little parental guidance is in order.

I confirm with the Chernobovs that Gregory is displaying what we might call the "phallic" or "Oedipal Conflictual Personality Phase" of development, precursor to the "genital" or "Oedipal Resolution Phase (IX)." He is just where he should be developmentally. The Chernobovs and I will work on parental harmony and leave Gregory free to resolve his own natural maturational dilemma.

One day the Chernobovs come to our appointment upset, reporting that Gregory has devastated his father so badly that Imre had a migraine for the first time in years. They tell me they were on their way out to dinner, when Gregory suddenly threw a full-blown temper tantrum. He couldn't stop crying long enough to tell them what was wrong. He clung to his mother like a baby, sobbing in agony.

"When he was calm enough to talk, he could only explain by saying he liked to go out with either of us separately but not with both of us together, because he 'didn't like to choose.' And he wouldn't or couldn't explain himself further."

"We know Gregory is working out a very normal oedipal relationship," I begin, and see them relaxing in their chairs. "We also know it is necessary for him to resolve this. All psychological lessons seem to build on each other, as they put opposites together into more abstract wholes, resolving conflict and moving personality growth forward so life is smoother and more satisfying.

"Theorists say that a son gives up his oedipal attachment to his mother because he fears retribution from his father, whom he also loves," I continue. "Consequently, he 'leaves' his mother, his first love, and 'identifies with his father, his second love' and his all-important male role model. Put that way, however, I think something is left out. I think the oedipal resolution is principally about learning to *share*. Three- and four-year-olds still think about relationships as infants and younger children do. They relate one-on-one. Gregory has clearly demonstrated that one-on-one is easier for him and that *choosing* is a miserable business. I believe he is in the process of learning that he can continue his strong and loving relationships with both of you. 'Choosing' *is* impossibly painful, because I believe he invests it symbolically with pre-oedipal meaning, and feels his choice is a permanent and irrevocable one, fixing his love and loyalty to one of you and rejecting the other. Of course he can't "choose" if this is what "choosing" means because he needs and loves both of you. You two remember that his choice is not what he fears. Express in your attitudes toward him that you can and will continue a close relationship. Simply give him love, room and time enough to make his developmental shift. Don't buy into his fears. Just let him work out his issues on his own."

This makes sense to the Chernobovs and greatly relieves Mr. Chernobov. Eventually, the whole process makes sense to Gregory, also, as manifested in a behavioral shift that demonstrates his increased comfort in sharing time with both his parents together.

Two of my favorite social workers, Gertrude and Rubin Blanck, have written thoughtfully on oedipal development. They say:

> Pursuing the theme that the oedipal level is a critical period, representing convergence of drive maturation and ego development, one has to think about it as occurring over a span of time.... The entry

point, the middle phase, and [the] temporary cessation of oedipal wishes that
take[s] place with entry into latency differ
in quality and intensity. (2)

So, following the intense Stage VIII of oedipal
conflict, the middle phase of Stage IX resolution allows
the child and his parents to help him learn to share: his
parents with each other and each of them with him. This is
the "Genital Personality," and *share* is the operative word.
Though sharing is almost never the critical term used for
the essential task of "Oedipal Resolution (IX)," it *is* the essential goal that "the convergence of drive maturation and
ego development" achieve.

Thirty-five-year-old Carolyn Levine and five-year-
old Gregory Chernobov are examples of the third position
on the first and second plateaus. Carolyn is at primitive
Stage III, while Gregory is a very healthy Stage VIII child,
at the conflicted phase of Freud's oedipal drama. Though
Stage VIII is an uncomfortable stage, the both/and "genital" personality of oedipal resolution is soon to follow and
is a much more pleasant position. From IX, the child or the
developmentally delayed adult can complete personality
unification at the fifth position (X), or the "Oedipal Integration Phase;" then, he can enter latency smoothly (Stage
XI of Autonomy) to consolidate his considerable emotional
gains. While my mother remains our fourth-stage example
on the first plateau, Gregory himself exemplifies two of the
three oedipal phases, VIII (conflict) and IX (resolution),
and he points us on toward X (integration), where he will

complete this critical and complex psychological task. And I repeat, for emphasis, passing these three oedipal phases, the individual solidifies his substantial emotional and psychological gains at "Stage XI of Autonomy."

Now we can examine a fully blossomed Stage IX personality and juxtapose her with Kenneth from the fifth position on the first plateau. Notice the plateau similarities and differences between these two. Edith, like Kenneth, comes to therapy with a relationship problem, but, ironically enough, she is troubled because her relationship is working a little too well. Edith and George have been best friends and lovers for many years. They take it for granted that they will eventually marry. Now, as she is finishing her final year in law school, Edith feels desperate. Next year is the year. George is finishing his graduate program too, and he has a Fulbright Scholarship that will allow them to spend a year in Italy. It is a dream come true. Both sets of parents are delighted, and wedding plans are in full swing.

"Well, all this sounds pretty good, and you even love the guy. So why are you here?" I ask, perplexed, and Edith begins to cry.

"I'm here because I'm afraid of living with George," she says. "We get along great. We have similar interests. We've spent enough time together over the years to know our relationship should work, but I'm afraid I'll lose myself in it. My parents were both 'super socially responsible do-gooders' who spent my whole childhood labor-organizing and lobbying for liberal causes and candidates' campaigns. I approved of their work. They never left me to babysit unless it was OK with me, and it always was. I felt quite special to have such important parents and to share in their good work. Though I never thought I resented it, I realize now it makes me afraid I will assume a similar role as George's wife.

"George has a strong personality. He believes in all the 'right' causes too, and of course that's one of the reasons I genuinely love him. Maybe you can see why I might be a little nervous about going to Italy alone with him. I've always kind of secretly—almost secretly from myself even—arranged my life so that George and I were in different cities. That way I could be myself and love George freely. Now I have to leave my external supports, and I'm not at all sure I have enough internal ones to remain my own person in the face of being with George full-time.

"George would have a hard time understanding why I feel this way. It's not him I'm worried about, it's me. I can just see myself gradually giving up the law, giving up everything, and becoming George's alter ego, like I was with my parents growing up. There was entirely too much harmony in our family."

Edith is so ripe for therapy that it does not take us long to bring some of her resentment and anger toward her parents into the open. Being overly responsible as a child has, to some extent, robbed her of a carefree childhood with enough time and energy to devote to her own development. Otherwise, Edith would have solidified her self-esteem so firmly that her love for George could not threaten it. Edith's story has a happy ending—as all stories should—because the developmental continuum sets human beings up to grow to completion, satisfied and happy. After several months in Italy, she writes that she is doing well. She does have her own life, and she also participates in George's. They are very happy, and she no longer fears losing herself. She has reached Stage XI of Autonomy.

The critical difference between Edith and Kenneth is that Kenneth thinks his loss of a sustaining partner will kill him, while Edith fears psychological damage, not death. Therein lies a whole plateau's worth of difference in intensity. It bears repeating that first-plateau material is external, intense, and fragmented, while that of the second plateau is internal, neutralized, and integrated.

Kara Bryan is our final example of a second-plateau personality. She also reaches Autonomy in therapy. She comes to consult me about Stage IX issues but rapidly understands the "groove" in which she is arrested. Having done this—much as Gregory Chernobov, freeing himself from an initial Stage VIII oedipal conflict, rapidly slid into resolution and integration Stages IX and X—Kara, solving her sticky Stage IX dilemma, moves quite naturally, almost effortlessly, though Stage X and into XI.

Kara has a highly dysfunctional background. Her father is an explosive and inconsistent man who terrorizes his family, bursting into rages without warning, screaming and lashing out physically, mainly at his children. Kara's mother looks the other way during these tirades, essentially denying what is happening. Kara feels her mother is always relieved that she is not the target.

The youngest by five years, Kara determines her life will be different from that of her two sisters. She manages to "hide out" in a large number of extracurricular activities, all of which keep her away from home most of the time. These activities also hone her talents and develop her repertoire of skills. She is in her school drama club and stars in most plays, which require endless rehearsals. She edits the school newspaper and writes articles for it. She plays flute in the school band. She is captain of the girls' soccer team, and she studies in the school library every day that she has free from these pursuits.

However, Kara has chosen a seriously dysfunctional young man as her boyfriend. Considering her background, it is not surprising. She is not happy in the relationship but cannot seem to end it. Arthur is a computer "nerd" who seems to fit the stereotype. He is also a workaholic, which may appeal to relationship-shy Kara. Arthur is a "case," but he *doesn't* get angry. More extreme even than Kara's mother, he is conflict-avoidant. I suspect it is this characteristic that appeals to Kara most. She has been willing to suffer the problems because Arthur is kind and gentle, but finally, following their first vacation in four years, Kara gives up. It is a disaster because Arthur cannot interact with Kara. Without "legitimate" excuses, he invents distractions. "Even if I'm never able to love anyone else, I know I can't live with Arthur," she states plainly.

Aside from helping her with her traumatic reaction to her father, my work with Kara is to encourage her to grieve the end of her relationship with Arthur. Although she has been truly convinced she will never love again, within a short while she meets an appropriate man who can share his feelings and be a solid partner in a relationship.

He is warm, funny, direct, and able to confront anything without making it a big deal. Very quickly he becomes Kara's best friend. She cannot believe she has spent so much time trying to extract a relationship from Arthur when hers with Henry happens so spontaneously.

Giving up Arthur proves that Kara is past her need for twinning in a relationship (Stage IX). She already has an observing ego in place when she comes into therapy, and now she is at the fifth position on the second plateau (Stage X) with a sound sense of her own worth as a separate person.

The evidence that Kara is still growing and is beginning to feel autonomous is clear in the way she handles Henry's expressing a commitment fear. She is disappointed, but she does not take it personally. "Whatever. Just let me know if you change your mind." She really means it. It isn't that she doesn't care; it is just that this problem has nothing to do with her. Henry's problem is his own. He will resolve it or he won't. If he does, great. If he doesn't, she knows their relationship can't work. As it turns out, he does resolve it. (Notice the difference between Kara and me in handling a failed relationship.)

Abigail Stevens is an adult personality from the first plateau who can be contrasted with Kara. Both are developed at their external cognitive and emotional layers of intelligence. At her core, Abigail is a "healthy" but still "Compliant Personality." She will no longer suffer insomnia, and she is free from suppressed anger, so she may advance beyond Stage VI in response to life experience. However, as we see her, she is not yet Autonomous (with a Stage XI core) like Kara, who can live happily with or without Henry and move freely about life's opportunities with a surety and an abandon that Abigail has not yet gained.

Kara dramatically demonstrates the utility of a strong observational ego in her rapid and solid growth to Stage XI mental health. And I have seen many times over that Piaget's model of cognitive structure, stage signature, and plateau transition works when applied to psychological/emotional diagnosis and treatment techniques.

Treatment Techniques

Each stage represents a particular relationship of the two psychic urges, roles, or personas with each other, and each best utilizes a different therapeutic approach. The stages evolve one into the next in a specific and orderly way. The evolution is as follows: Stage I's ill-defined, fragmented, or fused relationships require reality-testing therapeutic techniques to move on to Stage II's eclipsed, monolithic, all-or-nothing dynamic, which requires repression-lifting techniques (bringing the unconscious urge into awareness). This stage moves on to Stage III's mutually exclusive either/or paradigm, requiring advocacy for the unrepresented aspect of the psyche with the goal of producing twinship. Stage IV's twinship requires limit setting (and sometimes "ego lending") to establish the observational ego on the first plateau. Stage IV moves on to Stage V's rapid shuttling of attention between the last vestiges of ambivalence. It requires coaching (similar to Stage III's advocacy) so that the newly acquired observing ego can strengthen its position by keeping both sides of the issue in consciousness as the psychic system moves the urges closer toward final integration. With this focus, Stage VI inevitably unites the two urges. This integration automatically slips the system from a lower to a higher plateau, where Stage VI does its double duty consolidating sixth place plateau gains and inaugurating the first position on the following plateau via reality testing. At the second plateau this takes the form of separating a "my thought" from a "your thought." Each stage on the second plateau uses the same method for its evolution, as on the first.

Piaget's system of cognitive development and my application of it to emotional evolution shows how incomplete maturation along the first two plateaus of the psychic continuum comes from identifying oneself with partial aspects and concepts instead of with wholes. On the first plateau, the aspects are parts of the physical body, and on the second they are partial concepts of the psychological or representational self. A person comes to therapy because incomplete knowledge of his whole stronger, or higher self is painful and limiting. Therapeutic tasks expand immature or partial identity, bringing relief and satisfaction. But change itself is painful. Thus, even knowing that relief lies ahead, resistance to change is natural. Change is also frightening. Even when it is cognitively clear that the old ways are inadequate, taking on a new identity requires trust that there will still be a self—a recognizable self—when the old identity is let go and the new one is in place. As noted in the Introduction (page XVI) many people, overcoming their fear, make the transition to autonomy and find much more relief and pleasure at Stage XI than they experienced at other transitions throughout emotional evolution.

However, for those, like myself, who have had strong childhood spiritual tendencies, Autonomy brings with it a different experience. The relationship with the ego for people destined to proceed onto the third plateau is different. At Autonomy, the ego opposes progress. It resists further change because it suspects the truth: more change will eventually divest it of its power, a power which will be discovered to be illusory. While psychic growth *was* ego expansion, paradoxically, this freeing and empowering process readies the fully matured psyche for the spiritual work of ego *extinction*. I imagine it like an expanding universe which gradually looses the power to hold itself together. It leaves the personal ego vulnerable and breeds in it a most intense anxiety.

To halt growth here, for the spiritually inclined, would require an enormous amount of defensive and energy-consuming denial. Depleted and materialistic, the ego has nowhere to turn for inspiration or aid. By its very nature, all it knows and all it can seek is worldly replenishment, shifting and ephemeral, poor fare, indeed, for any journey worth making. Having spent twenty years outside spirituality, now I am thrust up against it at Autonomy by my fighting, but failing and faltering ego. Knowing I have grown, but knowing I am unfinished, I realize I must do something. I am desperate. I face what T. S. Eliot calls "the still point of the turning world...." (3) Unwilling and unable to go back, I recognize this as my essential life crisis, and I must find some thread of truth to lead me forward. Knowing only that what I seek is spiritual, I pray as hard as I know how to pray for insight and guidance.

PART III:

AT THE PORTAL OF SELF-KNOWLEDGE

CHAPTER 8:

Seeking Knowledge

Reading has its place, but I know it can take me only so far. My books say that people need teachers, gurus, and personal instruction. This is certainly the Vedic tradition, and it feels right to me. Most of the sages I've read about have been taught by gurus, but by now these teachers—as well as most of their students—have, as the Indians say, "passed." Of course I need a *living* master, and one who is fully enlightened. In addition, he must teach in *English*. From where I stand in my Brookline Village spiritual bookstore, such people seem in short supply.

But I start my journey here. As it is near my bank and the market where I shop, I go there often; it is a convenient place to browse, and it offers a wealth of material about what those teachers did teach while living. Whenever I go to this little village, I spend hours scanning the shelves and buy books by the pound. Any volume with an Eastern perspective on spirituality will do. My first choices include authors with vaguely familiar names, appealing jacket descriptions, with enchanting photographs of misty-eyed saints on the covers. Each time I come away with a backpack full of Krishnamurti; Ramana Maharshi; Nisargadatta Maharaj; Ram Dass; the Dalai Lama; *The Tibetan Book of the Dead*; Mouni Sadhu; Sri Ramakrishna; Krishnamurti's disciple Albert Blackburn; Nisargadatta's disciple Ramesh Balsekar; Paramahansa Yogananda; Muktananda; Muktananda's guru, Nityananda; and many books on Buddhism by Tibetan lamas, Indonesian holy men, and Zen masters. I even buy *The Course in Miracles*.

Despite living through the '60s, I am a decade older than that generation and am already working at a demanding job when it begins. Therefore, I do not go to San Francisco to participate in the New Age movement, but I do watch it with interest. Even so, I am a rank amateur in the spiritual field, not even knowing the difference between Buddhism and Vedanta. My choice of authors is random and eclectic. I concentrate at first on Tibetan Buddhism and on the Vedantins: Ramakrishna, Krishnamurti, Ramana Maharshi, and Nisargadatta Marahaj. I go to all the East/West conferences I can manage, including the one previously mentioned at Amherst, Massachusetts, in May 1985. Here, for the first time in the United States, the Dalai Lama reads aloud from the ancient Tibetan scriptures. They are in the form of highly decorated scrolls. They are impressive, and exquisite to behold.

His Holiness the Dalai Lama is far more impressive. He has a booming bass voice, and he laughs often, a resounding, spontaneous belly laugh. His expressive demeanor somehow conveys ancient peacefulness and fully ripened joy. He is definitely different from ordinary human beings. Once after a lunch break, before resuming, the Dalai

Lama looks up into the vaulted ceiling of the cathedral hall where we are gathered and points with pleasure as though to welcome something up above. He says, "One bird," referring to a bird that is settling in the rafters. We laugh, delighted at his discovery and even more with his wish to share it. I understand that he knows very little English at this time in his life, and there is something quite touching about his use of two words from his small vocabulary to communicate directly with us.

This fourteenth Dalai Lama is said to be enlightened and the reincarnation of his predecessors, all manifestations of the Bodhisattva or Buddha of Compassion. I have little or no understanding of reincarnation; even *enlightenment* is a vague term to me. I am told His Holiness lives on a spiritual plane called Nirvana, which means he is free from desire and suffering. Whatever all that entails, even my small exposure to him makes it easier—even mandatory—to believe in human development beyond the second plateau. I leave the conference with no more understanding of Nirvana or of enlightenment but with a great deal more confidence in my new study. This is truly a holy man who will not fit on either the first or the second platcaus. Therefore, there *must* be a third.

At this time, I am working as a psychotherapist at the Beth Israel Hospital in Boston, where I meet Ilan Kutz, an Israeli psychiatrist, who is also an artist and a creative thinker. Ilan is doing a behavioral medicine fellowship at the BI under the direction of Dr. Herbert Benson. Dr. Benson has already written his book *The Relaxation Response*, in which he studied meditating monks and advocates this technique as supplementary treatment for heart disease, asthma, ulcers, colitis, and other conditions exacerbated by stress.

Ilan works closely with Joan Borysenko, the psychologist, who has not yet made her national reputation. Joan and Ilan are preparing to teach a ten-week wellness course, which will include meditation, hatha yoga, and relaxation techniques. These groups are to be modeled on those already being conducted by Jon Kabat-Zinn at the University of Massachusetts Medical Center in Worcester. Joan and Ilan have designed their study to include an assessment of the efficacy of meditation as an adjunct to psychotherapy. Their hypothesis is that meditation, specifically the mindfulness meditation practiced by Tibetan Buddhists among others, will both hasten and strengthen the subjects' capacity for self-observation and so facilitate psychotherapeutic change. In mindfulness, deep relaxation and avoidance of obsessive or discursive thinking brings about an empty but alert mind, as opposed to the merely empty mind of the deep-sleep state. Mindfulness meditation enhances and clarifies one's mental processes. It also promotes self-discipline and the habit of introspection.

When I meet Joan and Ilan, this meditation/psychotherapy study is stalled for want of subjects. If I missed participation in the '60s movement, the conservative physicians at the hospital (where their psychiatry department is headed and staffed with Viennese immigrants immersed in the Freudian tradition) seem unaware of its occurrence altogether. They are reluctant to refer clients to what may seem to them an unscientific, perhaps even deranged, approach to therapy. There are at least a dozen clients in my practice who are willing to spend an evening a week for ten weeks to learn mindfulness meditation. So I refer them all, and the group begins. It is a huge success, and in addition, I have the pleasure of participating with Joan and Ilan in the data analysis and theory-building based on our results.

Our outcome study is published as the lead article in the January 1985 issue of the prestigious *American Journal of Psychiatry* (Vol. 142, Number 1). We conclude that meditation does indeed facilitate psychotherapy. A second critical benefit results from each client scheduling an hour of self-reflective time into his day. Self-reflection is the starting point for self-awareness, and self-awareness is the end-point for mental health. A number of my clients who begin meditation in this course continue the practice on a regular basis. When checking in with me over the years for one or another reason, they say meditation continues to be an important part of their daily lives.

Several personal results come from this study, too. I become good friends with Ilan and Joan. They introduce me to other people in the area who share our interest in Eastern thought and its application to therapy. One is a prominent Buddhist psychologist with a strong background in meditation and hypnosis. In the mid-1980s, he organizes a group of Buddhist therapists that meet once a month to discuss Buddhism's application to therapy. Although I am not a Buddhist—I have no new religious affiliation yet—I am keenly interested in the subject matter and participate in the group for several years.

As our interest in Eastern thought grows, Joan and

I decide to take an Indian guru-seeking trip together. We know that direct exposure to a living master is powerful. We plan a three-week trip in January 1987. Initially, we hope to meet several teachers and choose the best of them, but getting reliable information as to who is teaching where and when, and especially in what language, proves difficult. We are both busy, so we don't spend adequate time researching. Joan literally finishes revising the proofs of her first book, *Minding the Body, Mending the Mind*, just in time to board our flight. In the end, we fly to Mumbai (then still called Bombay) and travel south two hours by car to Ganeshpuri, where a friend of Joan's owns an apartment in the *Siddha Yoga* ashram compound. He is willing to let us rent it from the ashram. (We would have to rent some apartment from them in any case, and this guarantees us a place to live.) Therefore, we spend our first two weeks in Ganeshpuri at the ashram founded by Swami Muktananda in the mid-1950s. It is just a few miles from the ashram of his own guru, Swami Nityananda. Both of these men are now dead, and Swamini Chidvilasananda, or Gurumayi (Guru Mother), is the new heir to the *Siddha* linage. She is a strikingly beautiful Indian woman. Raised in this ashram, she and her brother—also named Nityananda--are groomed to become Muktananda's successors. Apparently, Nityananda is unable to handle the power his elevated status as a swami confers upon him, and he creates a scandal by seducing young women and collecting fast, flashy cars. Gurumayi is forced to defrock him in a special ceremony that strips him of his status as a swami.

During his lifetime, Muktananda gave what he

called "intensives," weekend instructional programs, to audiences throughout India, the United States, and other parts of the world. The *Siddha Yoga* movement has a strong following in America and a second ashram in South Fallsburg, NY. As his personal translator and the editor of many of his books, Gurumayi accompanies Muktananda on most of his teaching tours. Though I wish for exposure to some other teachers as well, I am looking forward to two weeks at one ashram and know that "guru shopping" does not provide adequate exposure to any teacher. Two full weeks at one ashram will allow for deeper study.

I have read all there is of Swami Nityananda's few published words and much of Muktananda's many. Nityananda, like Ramana Maharshi—about whom there are numerous volumes written, despite his own verbal reserve or, perhaps, precision—appears to have been a relatively silent saint or a man of few words. Apparently, in keeping with the *Siddha* tradition, his followers feel blessed in Nityananda's presence. Though I know Gurumayi has given a few intensives herself, I do not know her preferred teaching methodology, and I hope it will be of the more intensive and less of the blessings-oriented style.

When we arrive at the ashram, I am awed by the grandeur of the place. It is a well-constructed compound with half a dozen buildings for various purposes. The main building is a gorgeous three-story marble "palace" open to capture as much sunlight as possible. Palm trees grow inside the structure, adding to its spectacular beauty. The building's high walls and partial ceilings, while gracing the living "indoor" plants, also shelter the interior from the heaviest of the monsoon winds and rain. Polished black marble floors hold the cool of the night through the afternoon heat. Around the open courtyard are several stories of closed rooms in which the guru and her staff live. The building is altogether breathtaking, as are the grounds, gardens, and other structures. Rising like a mirage from the dusty, sun-baked Maharastrian earth, the ashram stands in full contrast to its surroundings. I can hardly believe this place is real and not a dream.

Joan and I are fascinated with India. We love the sights, sounds, colors, and unusual aromas. We find Indians warm and friendly people, with an uncommon sweetness. We love the center of Ganeshpuri, where Nityananda lived and is buried. His former house is now a museum. Despite the glory of the *Siddha* complex, for us, Nityananda's ashram is the most captivating spot in the area. We spend as many hours there as often as we can.

In contrast to the *Siddha* ashram, Nityananda's museum is a simple, boxy, one-story rectangle. It is constructed of thick clay bricks, finished with stucco. From a covered front porch, double doors open into a large, empty, meeting hall where hundreds of pictures of Nityananda and his devotees literally paper the walls. This hall occupies two-thirds of the building. Its high ceiling and few shuttered windows keep it cool throughout the day. At the back left of the hall, a door leads to an open porch, where the guru took his afternoon naps in the sun. Another doorway opens onto the back third of the building. One end of this long back room still contains the guru's chair where he sat to hold private audiences with seekers. At the other end are three bedrooms made of chest-high walls, with wooden poles arranged like bars, running from the top of the walls to the ceiling. These protect the occupants from stray animals while letting the cool night breezes into the sleeping quarters. Each of the small "cells" is furnished with a single narrow cot.

Joan and I are intrigued by the pictures. Most interesting to us is a series of close-ups of Nityananda's face as he lies dying. His expression is one of perfect peace and contentment. He seems totally absorbed in his experience, meditating upon it, drawing himself into it and it into himself, embracing death with blissful serenity.

Vijay, a guard at the museum, tells us that a realized master chooses his time of death. Usually, he says, when the master feels his work in the world is coming to an end, he will announce his readiness for *mahasamadhi*, sometimes specifying a particular day and time.

He tells us that the Sanskrit word *maha* is often used in compounds with other words, like *atma* which together, as *Mahatma*, means "great soul," Gandhi's title of respect. S*amadhi* means "union with God," which many people seek as the goal of meditation, while *mahasamadhi* means the ultimate joining of one's consciousness with that of the universal consciousness or death. Vijay tells us that enlightened souls in the Hindu tradition celebrate their deaths as joyful and natural experiences. Death is not shunned, feared, or denied as the Grim Reaper of Western lore symbolizes it.

Our favorite picture, the last in the series, shows Nityananda breathing his last out-breath. Throughout this series his eyes are closed, but even through his seemingly paper-thin eyelids, one can see that Nityananda's pupils are turning increasingly upward and inward toward that spot just between and above the eyebrows where Indian tradition locates the "third eye" of inner consciousness. In this last photograph, Nityananda's eyes are turned so completely toward this spot that they have disappeared altogether beyond their sockets. These pictures evoke in me the deep intuition that Nityananda is, indeed, profoundly and genuinely summoning his death. Near the third eye, in the crown of the head, is said to be a small aperture from which the subtle consciousness exits the body. It is dramatic to see this death scene photographed. Vijay finds a stool and opens a shuttered window for us so that we can photograph that picture in the darkened museum hall without using flash equipment.

Even though Indian culture is so thoroughly laced with spirituality, sadly many Indians whom we meet tell us that they do not know the meaning of their spiritual traditions and do not know the heart of the Vedic teachings. But even without knowledge, most Indians seem to retain a reverence for God and for spirituality, a sense that everything is a holy manifestation. Swami Tattvavidananda explains the reason for this is that all religions originating on the Indian subcontinent hold the creation and its creator as ever one, never separate. Therefore, if he were to ask "an illiterate farmer in a remote Indian village where *Isvara* (a commonly used name of God) is, he would, in turn, ask me where *Isvara* is not." (1)

Another facet of this spiritualism is giving shops

sacred names. Joan and I begin collecting them. There is Guru's Grace Laundry, Shiva's Bliss Tailor Service, Servant of God Petrol Station, Ramaswami (or God Master) Footwear, and Mahadeva (or Great Lord) Grocery. Like *Ganesha*, both *Shiva* and *Rama* are two other names for the One Non-dual *Brahman* that are very popular among Hindus. Even the taxi and lorry drivers decorate their vehicles each day with fresh flowers as an act of reverence and praise to God.

The jeweler's shop interests us because we have heard of the "sacred" radraksha beads. Davidatta, the jeweler, explains that these are seeds from a tree that, since ancient times, have been known as "Shiva's tears." These seeds are strung into necklaces of 108 beads called *malas* and used exactly like the rosary beads of the Catholic church, only instead of saying Hail Mary's, the Hindus recite 108 Sanskrit names of God, or repeat a chant or a mantra, the mala aiding meditative absorption. At one spot on the necklace, for orientation with closed eyes, there is a single bead that hangs down from the string. This is called the guru bead. On a rosary, a cross serves the function and occupies the position of the guru bead. In addition to serving as a practical aid to chanting or prayer, wearing "Shiva's tears" as a necklace is said to absorb negative karma. I had read that the rosary itself came from its use in the East and was brought to Europe by the Crusaders.

Joan and I get to know another resident of Ganeshpuri only slightly. He is Dr. Ruwalla, the local physician, and the least friendly or open Indian we meet. Thank God, or should I say Mahadeva, we don't get sick. The instruments laid out on white sheets in his operating room look too rusty and crude for vegetables or animals, much less for people. In addition to his medical practice, Dr. Ruwalla runs a bathhouse almost exclusively for women. This gives females access to Ganeshpuri's famous hot springs, which have mineral properties said to increase relaxation and enhance meditation, rendering the bather more receptive to spiritual blessings. I read that it was customary for Nityananda's devotees to bathe in the springs and then go to his house to meditate in his presence. If you are male, you may go straight to the springs to bathe. This is forbidden to women, since by long-established custom, men and women may not bathe "in any proximity even in bathing costume," Davidatta informs us. Dr. Ruwalla's compound—his office, hospital, and the three-roomed bathhouse—is located down a footpath behind Nityananda's temple. Each bathhouse room has a huge stone tub, some shelves for clothing, and a door that locks. Water from the hot springs is piped into the tubs. For two rupees, Dr. Ruwalla will fill the tub for you; and for three, he will even wash it out first. You can soak in this warm, pleasant smelling water that feels penetrating and healing on your skin, for as long as you like. Joan and I take many of these very relaxing baths. Then we go directly to meditate in Nityananda's museum.

There are no motorized vehicles in Ganeshpuri, but once we take a horse-drawn buggy to a temple several miles from the ashram behind which Muktananda's meditation hut still stands. The hut is perched high on a hill. We climb up the steep path to the hut at sunset. As we arrive at the top of the small "mountain," a breathtaking view of the whole valley lies before us. We can see the ashram, Ganeshpuri in the distance, and the river flowing behind the town and toward us along the valley floor. According to the autobiographical details of his enlightenment recorded in *The Play of Consciousness*, Muktananda saw red, then white, then blue lights when he meditated here. We meditate, too, but see only the yellows and pinks of the sun as it sinks behind the hills.

While I've always discredited "supernatural" experiences, like Muktananda's lights, I must admit that I feel the cement floor in Nityananda's house vibrate every time I go there. I can feel it against my bare feet as I walk in, and, when meditating, the vibration permeates my whole body. It is as though the electromagnetic field that holds my atomic structure together is excited, speeded up, coming apart, going haywire. This experience is not frightening; on the contrary, it is a profoundly pleasant sensation. I can imagine sitting there long enough to let all my atoms destabilize and spin off into intergalactic space, and I would have had no desire to stop them. Joan doesn't go in for "blue lights" either, but she feels the same sensations as I do in Nityananda's house. The floor, and eventually ourselves, vibrate electromagnetically here. We try, but we can't explain it. So we attribute it to the spiritual power of the holy man who inhabited this house for so long.

"What would happen to our consciousness," Joan muses, "if we sat long enough to unravel physically?" Since we never dissolve, we never find out.

"During those moments when disintegration feels most imminent," I tell Joan, " my consciousness does not feel altered, but it does feel different. It is, as always, watching, but watching differently then, with an attitude of special peaceful dispassion like the Ganeshpuri cows we see everywhere, wandering without restraint, munching sugarcane stalks." From what I know of psychology—though I am destined to learn much more about this critical subject—my consciousness, once established and reflecting in me, is changeless, so certainly, here, *what* it watches must make the difference, and that is an exceptionally quiet mind. It is the most profound relaxation I've ever experienced. So I accept for myself that the hallowed calm of the place where I sit is responsible for the special—even sacred—tranquility.

On one of our trips to the museum, Joan and I encounter a *sadhu*. India is full of *sadhus* or religious renunciates. We see many of them in Ganeshpuri, but only on this one occasion do we speak with one. For centuries *sadhus* have worn the same traditional unstitched orange costume. The top portion consists of a single piece of cloth worn over the shoulders or over the head and shoulders. This cloth is called an *angavasthram*, and the lower portion is called a *dhoti*. It is an ankle-length cloth that is wrapped several times around the waist and fastened there by a simple tuck. The renunciates' clothing is always orange, symbolizing the fire of knowledge which burns away ignorance. These two vestments, a pair of sandals, and a begging bowl are the *sadhus'* only possessions. He has renounced all else: family, communal obligations, and worldly pleasures in order to seek solely for spiritual knowledge. These, mostly men, are not unlike Catholic priests and nuns in the West, though often *sadhus* travel alone and do not belong to any religious order.

Our *sadhu* is doing what Muktananda did for twenty-five years when he wandered throughout India discoursing with various teachers and seeking enlightenment. The Hindu culture supports this lifestyle. It is considered a *papa* (or karmic discount) for a householder to refuse food to such a seeker when he presents himself for alms or *biksha*. And it is a *punya* (or karmic credit) for the householder to worship or give to God in this way.

Blinking into the blinding sun after a long meditation in the darkened museum, before our eyes can adjust, Joan and I almost collide with the *sadhu* seated on the porch enjoying its shade. We apologize and introduce ourselves. The *sadhu's* name is Swami Brahmananda, and he guesses correctly that we are Americans staying at the *Siddha Yoga Ashram*. He tells us he was born in Madras and had spent some time in Ramana Maharshi's ashram at Tiruvannamalai in the south Indian state of Tamil Nadu. Now he is traveling to an ashram in Gujarat.

"What are you learning at the *Siddha Ashram*?" he asks, coming quite directly to the point that is perplexing both Joan and me.

"Well," I say, "We chant the 'Guru Gita' each morning. (This lengthy song of praise to the teacher, written in Sanskrit verse, takes about an hour and a half to complete.) We find time to meditate daily, and we've attended a *yagna* (a ritual devotional sacrifice), which was quite impressive, but our chores take most of our time, and otherwise we sit in the presence of the Guru whenever she comes into the courtyard for *darshan*. I brought some books with me from

America, and I am learning from them, but that's about it. There's not a lot of teaching going on, unless you have money and time enough to pay the junior swamis for a lesson."

Darshan is a Sanskrit word that has a root meaning of "to see." In this case it connotes seeing the guru, being in her presence. During this time of personal exposure, the student pays respects and gives thanks to the teacher, while the teacher blesses the student. In the *Siddha* tradition, it is this exposure—students sitting with an enlightened teacher—that brings spiritual purification and eventual illumination to the student. The *Siddhas* hold that loving worship of the guru opens one's heart to the love of God.

Even though I try not to be disrespectful and show my real feelings about this *darshan* practice, I must have disappointment and incredulity written all over my face, because the swami bursts out laughing. His laughter is infectious. Joan and I begin laughing, too. We laugh until finally we are blinded by tears instead of sunlight.

When I get my breath again, I say, "We have come here to learn. Can you suggest anything that might help us?"

Swami Brahmananda gets serious then, too, and says that there are many ashrams in India and many, many gifted teachers who still use traditional teaching methods involving logical inquiry. So first of all, we should not despair. If we are serious seekers, then there will be teachers for us. "Rishikesh by the Ganges in the northern Indian state of Uttar Pradesh is the richest place to go for spiritual teaching," he says. "It is the city of the modern sages, and it abounds with ashrams and classes; and remember, no traditional teacher would charge for teaching."

"It may be a long time before I can return to India," I say. "Would you be willing to teach us something now?" The swami smiles his assent, and I try to think of the best question I can. After a moment, I give up. "I am such a beginner; I would need to start with what Vedanta teaches."

"To do justice to that subject would take a long time, but let me begin by saying great masters of the material of Vedanta study for many years to understand the core of the teachings, which is what you want to know. I am still studying."

Swami Brahmananda brushes at his very long and very gray beard, indicating that he has been at this task for quite some time. He looks to be in his fifties. He says that many masters of Vedanta do not stop learning after mastering the material for themselves. "In fact," he says, "instead of stopping there at personal satisfaction, many *sadhus* continue to study in order to become adept at teaching.

"Teaching is a serious business in Vedanta. The major message is one you have heard at the *Siddha Yoga Ashram*. It is even embossed on the banner in the front hall. It is the sentence, 'You are that.' Your problem is not that you haven't *heard* the message. Your problem is that you have not yet been instructed in *understanding* it. I am not a qualified teacher, but I can explain a few things. (2)

"First, *Tattvamasi* is an equation from the Chandogya Upanisad. It states that your true Self and *Brahman* are One. It is a *mahavakya* or short sentence, capturing the essence of the *upanishad's* message. Translated into English, you, or *Tvam,* and the Infinite, or *Tat,* are equal, *asi.* In fact, this entire universe, the manifestation itself, is One Whole which includes you and *Brahman*.

"If you've had no instruction this may be hard to understand, but a less well-known *mahavakya: Sarvam Khalvidam Brahma,* also from Chandogya may help you grasp it's meaning. This sentence states that the entire universe is the Devine. It includes the consciousness principle in all sentient beings and in all insentient things. The manifestation is one and all the seemingly disparate aspects of it, understood correctly, are One only. It is *'maya,'* or 'devine hypnosis,' as some are fond of saying, that gives the impression of many. In explaining this, teachers often analyze the things of the world first. Then the conscious being is examined. Phenomenal reality or worldly things are shown to be *objects* to your consciousness. They depend upon your consciousness for their appearance. They are therefore 'dependent reality' or *mithya*. All these objects can be reduced to parts. In the famous rope-snake example, the snake is obviously subjective, and so it is clearly understood as dependent reality. Even the rope, which is objective reality or *satyam* for the purpose it serves in the example, is really also *mithya* because it is made of fibers that come apart and, finally, exist only as concepts in your consciousness.

"Here, I will demonstrate dependent reality. If I take apart this flower, we will find, as with the snake and the rope, that there is no such thing as a flower at all." Swami Brahmananda picks up a yellow daisy-like flower that lay at his feet wilting in the sun, perhaps dropped there on its way to become an offering to the memory of Swami Nityananda. The Swami begins to take the flower apart, petal by petal and leaf by leaf, until all that is left on the ground where the flower had been before is a heap of parts.

"So you see," he continues, "there is no flower here. There are only petals, leaves, stems, and seeds. The flower has been reduced to parts with *different* names and forms, and these parts can be further reduced. A flower is not *satyam*. It is a *mithya* creation, and no dependent thing, nor its parts, can pass the *satyam* test for reality." Swami Brahmananda let the last of the petals fall from his hand and onto the pile of debris at his feet.

"A flower, like any other object, is only a *name* and a *form*. Finally, *flower* is a concept, the same as that rope, existing in someone's consciousness. As I've said, you can do this analysis for the whole universe, and all of it is *mithya*, relying on *your* consciousness for existence.

"'The being' or the 'you' in that *mahavakya* refers to all sentient beings. Through a series of logical steps, the teacher guides the student to see that the *you*, cannot refer to your body or to your mind but rather to your subtle essence, to awareness or consciousness, *the* subject that observes *all* objects, even those objects that we have previously and mistakenly assumed to be ourselves (the body/mind/sense complex). Consciousness is the only *satyam* or true reality. Only it can be shown to be self-existent, self-revealing, and non-negatable—the three qualities that define *satyam*.

"Vedanta doesn't talk of God, because that word immediately brings to mind some larger-than-life figure sitting in a heaven somewhere. Vedanta posits that the universe is created from the Source or consciousness itself, sometimes called *Brahmaji*. This Source operates just as dreams do. In both cases, the world of ropes and snakes and people and mountains exist in and of consciousness. In the *mahavakya*, the word 'That' stands for Universal Consciousness and since there is only one consciousness, *tattvamasi*, means your true self is *Brahman*, the whole. Just remember this: Presence/Awareness, or consciousness, 'The-One-Without-A-Second,' is omniscient, omnipotent, and omnipresent. This leaves no space for a separate self to exist *outside* of consciousness. So, *if* you exist, 'You *Are* That,' *tattvamasi*. *Do* you exist? You can't say you don't; can you? Therefore, as Ramana Maharshi used to say, 'Your head is *already* in the tiger's mouth."

Both Joan and I thank the swami profusely. I can't say I deeply grasp this Vedic summary, but no one had ever put so many fragments of the teaching together for me at once. Of course, this is a small part of the teaching, and I will have to think about it, let it sink in, and see how deep it goes. But, this is the apex of my Vedic learning so far, in India or at home. I see that hearing a teacher put it into words makes a far greater impact than does reading those same words in books. *And that last bit about the tiger's mouth is dramatic. I wish I could believe that. But, he said it like he really meant it! Why shouldn't I believe him? Maybe I can. At least I'll try and will give it serious attention.*

As for life and learning back at the Ashram, Joan and I continue to be disappointed. We dislike the feeling of the place. Most of the staff are attractive, young, blonde Americans. What kind of hiring practices can these be? Among this entourage, Gurumayi has her favorite devotees, "teacher's pets" we called them in grammar school. They are the only people who get close to her, along with any of the rich or famous who might swoop in from out of town. Among that group of staff members who are closest to the guru, there is a distinct and intense feeling of competition for most-favored status. In addition to this unpleasantness, we, the *paying* guests, have to work hard for eight hours a day at our assigned chores. Mine is housekeeping, which I dislike even when I have to clean my own house, and it is particularly unpleasant in the bathrooms of the Indian dormitories where the facilities are not used, but abused, and I am supposed to make them spotless again. Of course, I skip out as often as I can to bathe and meditate at Nityananda's museum.

Gurumayi never teaches once during our two-week stay; she only sits for darshan irregularly, making that public appearance to awaken our *shakti*. It does nothing for mine, I can assure you. I get more out of reading than out of being "blessed" in her presence. This ashram is run like a very lean and profitable business, not at all like a spiritual institution.

As for asking questions, forget it. You can't get close enough to the "teacher" for that. Silence reigns during her perhaps daily, but always erratic, public appearances. If one is able to ask a question, it has to be very short (and the answer possibly even shorter) because this conversation can only happen in the *darshan* line at the end of the public appearance. There will be fifty people ahead of you, hoping to ask a question, and another fifty behind, all waiting their turn to bow before the guru and be hit on the head by her wand of peacock feathers, supposedly another "blessing" from her.

I learn that this *darshan* practice is a form of Hinduism known as *baktiyoga*. *Bakti* is a Sanskrit word meaning "love," and y*oga* means joining. So in *baktiyoga* the disciple becomes one with the universe through love of the *siddha* or perfected one. Gurumayi had become enlightened through her devotion to her guru, Muktananda, and he through his devotion to Nityananda. Although it may have worked for them, it surely isn't going to work for me.

I don't even *like* Gurumayi, and I am certainly not going to be a *bakti* here. I resent not being taught, but most of all I dislike the poisonous atmosphere of the place. Family or group dynamics make it clear that the the pattern of relationship set by the "parent" filters down to become the emotional culture of the group. Here that culture is oppressive and unpleasantly competitive. And this is *before* I hear Gurumayi yelling at the deer in her deer park because they won't eat out of her hand. Like, who in their right mind would?

There is a pecking order, and it is clear who are the "haves" and who are the "have-nots." When I ask about it, if I *get* an answer, I am told that this harsh atmosphere, like the brutal *seva*, is especially and lovingly designed to break down my "ego," which is the main problem separating me from God. This is the Marine Corps boot-camp approach to spiritual training, and I don't buy it. It doesn't do a thing to break down my ego; in fact, it actually *increases* it because of the sense of victimization it creates, and it doesn't seem to be doing much for the staff, either.

I enjoy some of the other seekers. I certainly enjoy the town of Ganeshpuri and a lot of its people, especially Swami Brahmananda and his kind instruction. I enjoy

Joan's company and my meditations. However, when our two weeks are over, I am ready, happy to reclaim my passport—held at the ashram bank, lest a patron fail to pay some final fee—and I can't move fast enough to get to Bombay.

Bombay is clearly the India the traveler expects to find. Hordes of people jam the sidewalks and broad streets on foot, on bicycle, in three-wheeled auto-rickshaws, affirming Bombay as the overpopulated third-world city that it is. Snake charmers, organ grinders, beggers, and hustlers of all types who try to sell once-in-a-lifetime bargains stake out every street corner. In the Colaba section of the city, the palatial constructions of the Taj Mahal Hotel and the nearby British triumphal archway bearing the grand title "The Gateway of India," stand as reminders of the recently departed British Raj. Finally, beginning to come into its own, Mumbai's newly constructed skyscrapers affirm the city as independent India's affluent, international business and banking capital, which it is fast becoming.

As we travel during our third and final week—mostly by car because the airport at New Delhi is so often closed due to fog—Joan and I continue to read and to talk with people about Vedanta. In addition to the few books we brought with us, I bought one or two at God's Sweet Nectar Book Store in Ganeshpuri with titles I had not seen in my bookstore at home. Each teacher has a slightly different emphasis and often a radically different teaching style, but they all convey a similar message, and that is, "Know thyself as pure consciousness."

None of these Vedantins discredit other religions but go out of their way to see the validity of other points of view, including Christian mystics and saints, Jewish Kabbalists, Buddhists, and Sufis. They show a deep respect for spirituality, which they distinguish from institutional religion, and attempt to locate the common philosophical/spiritual point of convergence. One swami, Sri Yukteswar, Paramahansa Yogananda's guru, wrote a small volume entitled *The Holy Science*, in which he quotes extensively from the Bible and the teachings of Christ. In his introduction, he says,

> "The purpose of this book is to show as clearly as possible that there is an essential unity in all religions; that there is no difference in the truths inculcated by the various faiths.... But this basic truth is one not easily comprehended.... The creeds foster a spirit of hostility and dissention; ignorance widens the gulf that separates one creed from another." (3)

Given my particular contempt for the exclusive aspect of the religion I was taught as a child, the universality of the Vedic message is especially compelling. As I read more Vedanta, I become less interested in Buddhism, despite my great respect and fondness for the Dalai Lama and for Tibetan religious traditions in general. Vedanta, after all, had been Buddha's religion, too. Vedanta seems less complicated and more direct to me than what little I know about Buddhism.

Returning from a big trip you've looked forward

to for so long is always a letdown, no matter how much it might have met your expectations. This is especially true when you know you're going to be faced with dozens of messages, piles of unopened bills, and a host of angry clients who felt abandoned by you for the three weeks you were away. As we buckle our seatbelts for takeoff in Mumbai, Joan and I look at each other knowing we both have the same thought: *It was a lot more exciting when we buckled in at JFK anticipating India.*

I'm not ready to leave. I have just begun to explore a culture, a set of traditions, and a body of wisdom that fascinate me. India feels more like home than like a foreign country— *seva*, beggars, disappointing teachers, fogged-in airports, and all. I fully understand the appeal of *sannyasah* and would like to spend the rest of my life seeking knowledge like Swami Brahmananda. If I could think of any way to pay the mortgage and my daughter's tuition other than by returning to work, I would grab an orange parachute and bail out on the spot, but, much against my wishes, I know I have to go home.

Now, I must be contented with that dry reading again. It feels like a serious handicap to have to learn Vedanta from books. At least in India almost everyone is interested in the subject no matter how well or poorly they understand it, and Joan and I talk about Vedanta with almost everyone we met. I don't know anyone in Boston with whom I can discuss it, except for Joan, of course. If I were Buddhist, thanks to the Dalai Lama, I suppose, Westerners would know I was referring to a religion when I spoke of Buddhism. But Vedanta? Most people I know have never heard the word.

CHAPTER 9:

"When the Student Is Ready, the Teacher Appears"

After reading more works by and about enlightened Eastern saints and after a second trip to India looking for one, I have little hope of success, but I continue exploring. Dr. Richard Maurice Bucke's *Cosmic Consciousness*, published in 1901, expands my search beyond the East. I learn that this book is an early and well-respected study of spirituality. Bucke chronicles the lives of fifty people whom he considers enlightened. He includes Christ, the Buddha, the Apostle Paul, Plotinus, Mohammed, Dante, William Blake, Walt Whitman, several English poets, and a few men of God from the Church of England. He studied only one Vedantin, Ramakrishna, but the book's special interest to me is precisely that it extends my awareness of enlightened people to Westerners. I know almost nothing about them, and this book opens the spiritual "New World" to me.

Once discovered, I am astonished to learn how many successful seekers wrote their memoirs to guide their still-struggling disciples toward union with God. I begin reading the voluminous works of St. John of the Cross, St.

Teresa of Avila, Saint Francis of Assisi, and many others. Then, in the bookstore of a monastery in Western Massachusetts a book fairly falls off the shelf into my hands, and so I discover Evelyn Underhill's *Mysticism,* the unparalleled classic of Western luminaries. Using the mystics' own testimonies—some that she translated herself from Latin, Greek, and various other European languages—Underhill carefully details the lives of nearly a hundred protestant and Catholic saints going back to medieval times. She synchronizes their disparate pathways into one uniform staging system. And even though their experience and her stages mesh most astonishingly and precisely with the design of my still empty third plateau, her findings will not "live" for me until I can study a few "case examples" myself. Even more than with Autonomy, in order to sort and arrange stage dynamics on the third plateau, I must study real people on those rungs of the ladder. Without careful scrutiny, I can neither affirm this ultimate state as genuine, nor describe it with any clarity. Even though the Dalai Lama made a third-plateau believer out of me, I only *saw* him. I do not *know* him.

In the spring of 1987, an old acquaintance telephones. Vitalbhai is an Indian pharmacist who lived in Nairobi and whom I met many years earlier while traveling in East Africa. He is in Boston en route to Canada to visit his now adult children in college. We meet for tea to update each other on the past twenty years of our lives. Though not a religious man himself, now knowing of my interest in Hindu philosophy, as we say good-bye, Vitalbhai remembers something and goes to his car. He returns and hands me a pamphlet that a friend had forgotten in his backseat. The pamphlet, titled *Action and Reaction*, is written by a Swami Dayananda Saraswati, whom neither of us know. The cover of the booklet informs me that Swami Dayananda has an ashram in Pennsylvania.

I read the pamphlet and like it. It compares human beings to actors who play many roles on stage but who nevertheless remain the same essential person throughout all their various parts. The pamphlet also says that a person identifies with many aspects of himself—his thoughts, his emotions, his body—but, since all this changes regularly, his real identity always remains the pure unchanging witness consciousness. This simple explanation of the unifying and objectifying effect of the witness consciousness could help clarify the inevitable struggle my clients have with their own psyches. It underscores the critical importance of objectivity (or discrimination) in promoting insight into one's self and sharply differentiates sound judgment (or dispassion) vs. subjective emotionality in evaluating situations and in making decisions. *Action and Reaction* closes with a simple and practical meditative exercise to facilitate healthy ego detachment. Knowing it will be helpful in my work, I order a dozen pamphlets from Pennsylvania. My name is obviously added to the mailing list, as, in a short while, I receive a flier announcing that Swami Dayananda is to give a day and a half talk at MIT in June.

On the designated morning, I go to Cambridge to attend the lecture. It is exactly six months since my second trip to India in search of a teacher. I have no idea what to expect, but my many disappointments by any number of swamis, in India, and later in the United States, leave me apathetic. I've worked very hard and found very little. I know from my Buddhist friends, some of whom have traveled in the Far East, that living masters in all traditions still exist, but I haven't found anyone who, literally and figuratively, speaks my language.

It is a perfect June day, gloriously bright, exquisite. The sky is its deepest blue, without a wisp of cloud. A cool breeze modifies the sun's heat, which, even before nine on this morning, would otherwise be intense. The Cambridge side of the Charles River, just at MIT, where Massachusetts Avenue intersects Memorial Drive, affords the best possible view of Boston. From this vantage point, with the Hancock and Prudential buildings taking their places next to the golden-domed State House atop Beacon Hill, the city's skyline is magnificent. Today, a hot sun, crisp air, and the brisk breeze make ideal sailing conditions in the Charles River basin, and Boston's Community Boathouse has launched its fleet. The small sailboats ply their courses back and forth across the river. White sails and little wavelets sparkle in the sunlight. The air smells clean and fresh. This is the Boston I had fallen in love with as a young woman in graduate school. This is Boston at her best.

I hate to leave the river for any reason, but I especially hate to leave it in exchange for the dark maze of hallways that connect MIT's complex of buildings. As if dark, dingy, and confusing were not enough, these labyrinthine tunnels seem perpetually filled with fumes from lethal chemical waste, because, undoubtedly, that is exactly what I am inhaling. Given my poor navigational skills, I force myself inside early to allow time for groping through the sulfurous corridors to locate the lecture hall.

Miraculously, I do find the room with almost no trouble. In fact I am the first person to arrive. The lights aren't even on. It is a large lecture hall in which the rows of desks descend from the back of the room toward the central lecture pit furnished with a blackboard, a lectern, and a large conference table. I choose a seat directly in front of the podium but in the second row. I don't quite dare to sit totally exposed in the first row. Swamis still make me nervous.

With a few minutes to spare, I decide to locate the nearest restroom. I mark my chosen seat with a notebook and set out in search of one and, again, miraculously find it nearby. When I return to the hall, one other person has arrived. He is sitting by himself, lounging in the front row by the door, to the right of the podium. He is wearing swami-orange and has a long gray beard. His legs are stretched out, as if to rest them from a cramped car ride. This must be Swami Dayananda. But he is alone, unprotected by an entourage of devotees. Except for his beard and unusual dress, he could be anyone waiting as I am for the talk to begin. I have trouble accepting the obvious because of my past experience with pompous gurus. However, this *must* to be Swami Dayananda. Remembering that his picture is on the flier on the seat with my note paper, I walk past him, take my seat, and compare him with the photograph. That's him, all right; Swami Dayananda, for sure. If nothing else, his being alone is a first. A swami without pomp and circumstance, without court and ceremony, an informal, down-to-earth swami, without anyone trailing along behind carrying peacock feathers! This alone gives me a degree of hope.

Soon a maintenance crew arrives with a microphone and speakers. They make a quick *namaskar* to the swami (an Indian greeting, consisting of putting both palms together under the chin, briefly bowing the head, and saying "namaste," which means, "The God within me greets the God within you") and start setting up their equipment. Gradually other people enter. Some obviously know the swami and greet him warmly. Some chat with him briefly. He is cordial and informal, as they are. I notice the swami makes a special point of greeting the children who come in with their parents. He asks their names and says a few words to each child. Outside the hall I hear people setting up tables and bringing in dishes of food for lunch. The aroma of Indian spices is divine. This special combination of aromatic fragrances reminds me of my best meals in India.

The president of the MIT Indian Students' Association introduces Swami Dayananda, whom he says needs no introduction because everyone—except for me, I presume—knows him already. He says we are most fortunate, as it is very unusual to have a teacher of the swami's caliber in the U.S. for a few months each year. He adds that we will break for tea in two hours and for lunch in four.

Swami Dayananda walks to the podium, stands there for a moment in silence, and then begins his talk with this sentence: "We have in our understanding three types of reality."

Good Lord! I think. *Another first. This man is be-*

ginning a twelve-hour seminar with the heart of Vedanta's ontological message. This isn't going to be another Sunday school lesson, such as I've heard so often during my search. Swami Dayananda is clear and concise. He speaks without notes, using simple English words, presenting lively images and effective metaphors. A complete novice could attend this lecture and understand the essential message of Vedanta.

With all that, he is funny, too. He could be a professional comedian. Although his message is deadly serious, he keeps his audience intensely engaged in learning and laughing at the same time. It doesn't take long for me to recognize that I won't be disappointed this time. Here, at last, is a genuine teacher, and I already know that he could be my teacher, having appeared, I presume, because I must finally be ready.

Swami Dayananda teaches traditional Vedanta using Vedic examples handed down from generation to generation for several thousand years, (1) first through an oral tradition and, later, written on palm-leaf manuscripts, kept together as "books." Much abbreviated and with little of his humor showing in my rendition, the lecture goes something like this: (2)

"When I ask you to identify a clay pot, many people will say, 'That is a pot.' Someone else might say, 'That is clay.' Which answer is right? You could say both are right, but if the words are not synonyms, then one must be more correct than the other. So which is more correct?

"The more correct answer is clay, because clay is the substance of pot. *Pot* is only a name and a form imposed upon clay. Similarly, golden ornaments exist because of gold. They assume many shapes and appearances, but there is only one substance on which they depend for their existence. The necklace comes from a lump of gold. It exists because of gold, but the jeweler could melt it down, if he wished, to make bangles or earrings.

"Neither the pot nor the ornaments enjoy a self-existent reality, yet they cannot be said to be nonexistent. The horns of a hare are an example of nonexistent reality, called *tuccham* in Sanskrit."

This—like the other two examples—is familiar from my reading translations of the ancient Vedic texts. We are getting a classic lecture, and this pleases me since I've never heard one.

"But pots and golden jewelry do exist. However, even though they exist, they have a dependent status in reality. The Sanskrit term for dependent existence is *mithya*. There is not an English translation for this word, so we are stuck with the Sanskrit.

"Anything which really exists, like the clay and the gold in the examples, anything which enjoys an independent reality, is known in Sanskrit as *satyam*. To qualify as satyam, a thing must satisfy three conditions. It must be (1) self-existent, it must be (2) self-revealing, and it must be (3) non-negatable.

"When you apply the *mithya* and *satyam* criteria for existence to objects in the world, including the clay and the gold of our examples, what happens? Everything that is 'put together' can and will come apart. Trees can be reduced to trunks, roots, branches, and leaves. Flowers to

petals, leaves, and stems. These parts of objects can be reduced further to cells, to atoms, and finally to quantum particles. In this kind of analysis, every object in the universe
can be reduced until all that is left is a name and a form, a
concept.

"Take your clothing, as another example, but be
careful, you may lose your shirt. Cloth can be reduced to
material and then to thread. Thread can be further reduced
to yarn, and then to fiber, and, like the parts of the tree,
fibers can be further reduced. Take your body as an even
more intimate and compelling example. It too can be reduced to skin, muscle, flesh, bone, and various organs.
These can be further reduced to cells, then to atoms, and
finally also to quantum particles.

"So is the quantum world reality? Is it *satyam*?
The quantum itself depends for existence on human concepts. And modern physics tells us more. It says that by
measuring the quantum, human intervention causes a quantum wave, which has several potential forms, to give up
its wave status and take one or another specific form as
a quantum particle. So the quantum does not seem to enjoy an independent existence either. Therefore, neither the
quantum world nor the entire world of classical objects,
including your own body, is *satyam*.

"Is anything *satyam*? As before, with the clay pot,
let's begin with something commonly known. Let's begin
with you as a conscious being. That you are conscious is
clear. No one had to tell you this, and you never doubted it
either.

"Being conscious implies having various means of knowledge, the five senses of perception, and a reasoning mind that can extend those sense perceptions by direct or indirect inference. These various means of knowledge account for all your personal information about the entire universe. Therefore, like pots and jewelry, trees and the human body, all the objects within your universe, are *mithya* objects. But, you, the 'I,' or consciousness may be different. 'I' is self-evident. And anything that is self-evident is also self-existent, so if it can pass the 'nonexistence' test, 'I' might qualify as *satyam*.

"Now we may have two classes of things. We have the entire *mithya* world of dependent reality, and we have the self-evident and self-existent 'I' that is different and that may be *satyam*. Where does this 'I' start and the universe stop? What is the point of demarcation between the two?

"There is generally a great deal of confusion about this because we take as 'I' anything that has about it an 'I-sense.' Therefore, I never confuse myself with the sun, the moon, the sky, with my immediate neighborhood, with other people, with my house, my car, or even with my clothing. But beginning with our own bodies, starting at the skin and proceeding inward, here we get into trouble. In language we acknowledge this confusion, and our personal identification of 'I' with our bodies, in such statements as 'I am black,' 'I am fat,' 'I am short,' 'I am blonde,' or worse, 'I am bald.'

"I perceive the entire universe outside my own body as objects of my perception. Even your body, I perceive as an object, and you perceive mine similarly. Nevertheless, we have great difficulty acknowledging that our own bodies are also objects to consciousness. Despite actually seeing all bodies, *including* our own, as objects like any other, and despite the fact that perceiving them *objectively* necessarily makes them separate from the *subjective* consciousness that is perceiving, *still* we have trouble accepting that our bodies are not ourselves.

"Notwithstanding our special relationships with our own bodies and the 'I-sense' that pervades them for each of us, our bodies are clearly objects, evident to the 'I' and not self-evident. Thus, bodies are *attributes* of 'I' and not its *substance*, just as thoughts and feelings are revealed as objects to 'I.'

"We started with you as a simple conscious person, and now we have 'consciousness,' which is the 'I,' standing alone as the only possible self-evident thing. Your body, as well as all the contents of your mind—all your thoughts and feelings, not to mention the whole universe, including time and space—reveal themselves only to the conscious 'I.' 'I' depends on nothing but itself for its existence, whereas only your consciousness of them confirms the existence of objects.

"With the 'I' being self-evident and self-existent, let's apply the test for negation to determine if 'I' qualifies as *satyam*. Is the 'I' ever absent? It exists in the waking state, it exists in dreams, and it exists even in deep sleep. If your consciousness did not persist throughout deep sleep, how would you know when you awakened that you had slept well? Have you personally ever experienced nonexistence? You cannot claim that. Even the statement 'I do not exist' only proves that there is an 'I' that asserts it does not existence.

"You might say to me, `Well, I exist now, but one day I will die and cease to exist.' And, I must answer by saying, again, you are confusing your body, an object, with your true essence, which is consciousness. Objects, like bodies, are observed as existing in time and so will eventually die. But your body is not you, and time is a concept that exists within consciousness, just as your body does. The conscious *you* exists neither in your body nor in time. Instead your body and time exist in it.

"Let's look at time for a moment. When you think of the past, those thoughts always appear in the present moment. Likewise thoughts of the future always appear in the present moment. In fact, there is nothing that does *not* appear in the present. Consciousness is always present. So consciousness, then, *is* non-negatable. And now we have one thing that is *satyam*. It is consciousness. It is the 'I,' and that 'I' is 'you.'"

I am following the lecture with intense interest. Consciousness, now established as beyond one's body, beyond all bodies and beyond all minds as well, brings us to the logical edge of my own personal question. "Why am I, *me*?" had been one of my frequent childhood conundrums. "Why is my consciousness in this body and my mother's, for example, in hers? How did she get locked into that body and I into this one? How does awareness become split up like that and arbitrarily assigned to individuals?" As a child, I would think about this until I was dizzy and, getting nowhere, had to stop.

As these thoughts flash through my mind, the swami is still lecturing. I must be listening with "visible" attention because it seems possible that this lecture might answer my big question, and, looking directly at me, Swami Dayananda continues.

"Now comes an important question. Can the consciousness that is all-pervasive for you be many, or is it one. We know that if you die, the world will continue to exist. We know that every night when you go to sleep, the world remains, and it is still there in the morning when you awaken. So are your glasses, if you can remember where you put them."

The Swami continues to speak as though to me alone. He keeps his gaze fixed on mine, and he seems to give the subject special attention because my whole demeanor bespeaks its critical importance to me.

"Here your problem with the concept of a single unity consciousness *still* emanates, as always, from the *deep* and *habitual confusion* of taking yourself to be your body/mind/sense complex and especially as the content of your thoughts instead of knowing yourself as pure consciousness alone.

"Listen to this carefully," he says, continuing what seems to be his very personal address to me. "Your puny little individual consciousness includes—it even *establishes*—the existence of time as we just saw. It establishes the existence of *space*, as we shall see in a moment, and of the entire universe as we shall review once more. Your consciousness does all of that. And so does mine! Now, can we draw a line between your consciousness of the universe and my consciousness of it? Is my consciousness of time, of space, and of the universe different from your consciousness of these things? What we know about our conscious perceptions may be different, but our conscious perceptions themselves are not different. How could they not be linked?

"Let's take space. In order to comprehend space, consciousness must have no circumscribed form. It must be spatially limitless. Space is space-consciousness. The whole concept of space, and your perception of it, exists within consciousness and not the other way around.

"For the sake of argument, let's suppose there is some object that is outside space and so outside of your individual consciousness. Between consciousness and that point outside consciousness, there is distance, is there not? What is distance due to? It is due to space. All distance is spatial. So between consciousness and any point in space, is there not distance, and where does that distance show up? It shows up in your consciousness, which is beginning to look a lot less insignificant now. Is there distance between a star and consciousness? No. What is the distance between the entire universe of space and consciousness? Zero. Even space relies on consciousness alone for its manifestation.

"So consciousness is not spatially limited any more than it is temporally limited. Space itself exists within consciousness just as time does. How could consciousness be limited in any way and at the same time encompass the vastness of space/time perceptions and concepts, as well as the universe— all physical matter and energy, the planets, stars, galaxies, intergalactic space, black holes and all seen, unseen or imagined entities?"

Swami Dayananda's synthesis of the material with which I have struggled for so long is crystalline. He pulls much more of it together for me in more detail than Swami Brahmananda had time to do in Ganeshpuri. I am already accepting the irrefutable logic of these arguments more completely than ever before. At an intellectual first layer of knowledge, the message is becoming whole, and this last "personal" interchange on the vital subject of the unity of consciousness is making it *feel* more real to me at deeper psychic layers. Then Swami Dayananda comes up with his next analogy, and this one hits me very near the solar plexus of core knowledge.

Still looking directly and intently at me, he says, "Think of it this way. Again for the sake of argument, let's suppose there is such a phenomenon as ESP (extrasensory perception), and let's suppose that you and I both have it. Now my thoughts are as clear to you as they are to me. And your thoughts are as clear to me as they are to you. Now what happens to consciousness? Is it divisible? Or is it one?"

I am stunned. I can feel myself taking a step up the ladder toward core knowledge of unity consciousness. This series of big "answers" to my major personal questions allows me to see consciousness as "one" for the first time. I watch myself settle into that new and deeper understanding.

Why is the ESP example so electrifying for me? I think its power lies in my understanding empathy. Every day, my work involves using this psychic tool. I fully accept it as quite scientific and as absolutely real. There is nothing magical about it, and mine has always improved, stage by stage, as I've matured throughout my lifetime. Everyone's capacity for empathy improves as they mature because this capacity expands in tandem with self-awareness. It is Piaget's "assimilation/accommodation" principle. Increased empathy or seeing the world more clearly from another person's perspective always improves relationships with others. In fact this is one of the most important goals and benefits of psychological maturation.

While empathy is an understandable phenomenon, I have always thought of telepathy and ESP as something quite different, magical and unscientific. The swami's example invites me to look at it differently. Perhaps telepathy *can* be seen simply as the high end of an empathy scale. I have never thought of it like that. If people did have "high end" empathy or "mental telepathy," then, conceivably, all objects, now clearly including all thoughts and feelings, would exist within one general "sea of consciousness." This makes the idea of unity consciousness less bizarre and vague to me.

I still have many questions, of course, and I know I will have doubts. I am way down the ladder from stable, uncomplicated, deep core knowledge of unity consciousness, but I feel myself viscerally relax into it now, and this is a brand new feeling. Now I know a lot more about spiritual maturation and catch a glimpse of what enlightenment might be. I feel confident that enlightenment is a deep truth and that, eventually, it can be understood. Swami Dayananda looks as though he knows it to his core.

As I relax, the Swami's attention transitions from

me to the audience as a whole. Occasionally, I notice him pay specific attention to other individuals. Like many highly skilled teachers I have known, he has a keen, seemingly near "telepathic" sense of his listeners. He never loses the thread of the lecture, but like a heat-seeking missile, he takes little "detours" to address the needs of particular individuals within the group. I haven't done much lecturing myself, but I presume this skill of attending and responding to nonverbal cues in an audience is like noticing in conversation when someone's attention is focused and when it drifts away. I assume this skill is part of what makes Swami Dayananda an especially gifted teacher.

"So you are really consciousness," he continues. "In Sanskrit, *saccidananda* is a compound word, and a *mahavakya,* a key sentence, that summarizes the whole meaning of Vedanta. Self-revealing awareness is *cid* or *cit* or the 'I' of 'I Am,' and presence, being, or existence is *sac or sad* (*satyam*). This is the 'Am' of 'I Am,' and *ananda* means limitless. The words in a Sanskrit compound modify each other. So *saccidananda* means 'I am limitless-consciousness-being.' And there is only *one* consciousness. One *satyam*. To make it crystal clear, we sometimes call it 'The One-Without-A-Second'. This consciousness is who you are. So how could you fear or despair? There is no *other* to hurt you, and you are already all you could ever seek to be."

Swami Dayananda breaks off the Saturday lecture and says we will resume here the next morning. On Sunday, he reviews the major themes from Saturday and says, "In Vedanta, we try to avoid using the word *God* because of the connotations it brings with it of a big fatherly figure in the sky or in some heaven. This view would destroy the very essential Vedic principle that you and God are one as stated in the *mahavakyas*: *ayamatma brahma,* meaning *atman* and *brahman* are one, or *aham brahmasmi,* meaning I am *brahman.* Instead, we use the name *Isvara,* which means "the intrinsic ruler of the universe," the author and executor of all its laws and orderly functions. Thus we say that *Isvara* is the maker *and* the material of the universe.

"In most creative activities," he continues, "the maker and the material he uses are different. The potter uses clay; the jeweler, gold; and the tailor, cloth. But, in the special instance of creations within consciousness the maker and the material are the same. In this case the maker can never be separate from creation, and the creation is a direct manifestation of its creator. The clearest example of this is our dreams, in which we create whole worlds out of the only material we have, which is consciousness. This is what we postulate as the universe that exists and is created by *Isvara's* consciousness. (3)

"Before the potter, the jeweler, the tailor, the dreamer, or any other creator, creates, he has some knowledge from which his creation arises. So before universal creation, we infer there was universal knowledge. Knowledge always exists within consciousness and so depends upon an intelligent being. The intricacy, the order, and the invariability of the scientific laws in the universe imply intelligence at work in its design. It would be hard to image all of this order coming randomly out of chaos, purely by happenstance, without a plan, and without prior knowledge.

"Since your essence is also consciousness, this makes you one with *Isvara*. Now, *Isvara* is the material of the creation, and, you *are* the creation. Thus, the truth of the equation, 'You are that,' or *tattvamasi*, another of the *mahavakyas*—or key sentences, like *saccidananda*—which reveal the essence of Vedanta. You are that, not because you are omnipotent or omniscient, but because your essence is *saccidananda*, the only self-evident, self-existent, and non-negatable element in the universe.

"Your unity with the source is not something you must *experience*; instead it is something you must *know*. Here is where many modern Vedanta teachers make one of several fatal mistakes. They tell you that you must experience your oneness with God rather than *know* it."

Here my ears perk up again. I have suffered through this fatally mistaken interpretation by most of the Vedanta teachers I have met. Muktananda's *Siddha Yoga Ashram* in Ganeshpuri is very big on experience instead of knowledge. Swami Dayananda holds a refreshingly reasonable and quite different point of view.

He continues, "You experience your consciousness in all states—waking, dreaming, and sleeping, so you experience it continuously. You have plenty of experience of your consciousness. More will not solve your problem. The problem is *ignorance* of what you experience, and this problem can only be resolved by *knowledge*.

"You are Unity Consciousness already and, so, one with the Creator. But you have to *know* that you are this conscious oneness. Otherwise you can go through life suffering and seeking and never understanding that you already *are* what you seek to be. Nothing needs to be added to you. Nothing *could* be added. There is nothing you must do. There is only ignorance to be lost. Rather than asking if you can find *Isvara*, you should ask, instead, if you can escape *Isvara*. Ignorance alone covers your true identity.

"Finally, *saccidananda* itself remains unmodified by any of the changes it registers. Just as clay remains clay and gold remains gold before, during, and after being fashioned into various forms, so you remain pure consciousness throughout all your gross or subtle modifications. Before the creation of your body and brain, you were one with *Isvara*, during your manifestation as this body and brain, you are one with *Isvara*, and after your body dies, you remain one with God as you always were; for you are not the dead body; you are the consciousness that reflects in that body while it is healthy enough to support the reflection. Consciousness was never born and will never die. Emphasizing the indestructibility of consciousness, Lord Krishna says in the second chapter of the *Bhagavad Gita*, 'The sword cannot cut it. Fire cannot burn it, water cannot wet it; neither can it wither in the wind.' (4)

The lecture is over. There is time for questions. Several people ask for clarification of various theoretical points. A few ask practical questions about child-rearing, about the problems Indian parents face with their teenagers who have grown up in an American culture that is alien to that of their parents and to the culture in their homes.

"Swamiji?" I ask, adding the suffix "ji" to an Indian name or title is a sign of respect. "Would you say more about the mistaken emphasis of 'modern' Vedanta teachers who talk of experience instead of knowledge?"

Swami Dayananda says that this experience/ knowledge mistake is a very big and problematic one. He says it follows from wrong translations of Sanskrit into English and into other Indian languages. "I mentioned during the lecture that *ananda* can be translated in two ways. Its meaning in the compound *saccidananda* is clearly limitless. However, another meaning for the word is fullness or even bliss. You can only know which meaning is correct if you have studied the traditional texts themselves instead of relying on translations. Less scholarly translators have often chosen to define *ananda* as bliss. Now you can see the problem."

I can't, but fortunately he keeps going with his explanation. "If you use the wrong definition and focus on bliss, you immediately find yourself on the wrong path in the roadway searching for an experience. Bliss, after all, is a feeling, an experience, and in searching for an experience, you are no longer on the traditional and correct path addressing a deeper understanding of the meaning of consciousness as limitless. I refer to this as a mistake made by modern Vedanta teachers because the traditional teachers never made it. Like many mistakes, this wrong notion that Vedanta advocates a bliss experience, instead of addressing the problem of ignorance, seems to have become a popular fad, especially among Vedanta teachers who come to the West. That's why I make the distinction between *modern* and *traditional* Vedanta. There is only one Vedanta, but now the distinction has to be made between a right and a wrong interpretation of the teachings."

This clarifies my question and implies that much of my personal "suffering" at the hands of modern Vedanta teachers arose, again, out of ignorance. After Swami Dayananda concludes the lecture, I join the line of people who go up to thank him. I tell him I am immensely grateful for this lecture and that I have found his talk profoundly helpful.

Everything about this swami implies he is genuinely open, completely nonjudgmental, and totally unpretentious. At the same time he seems fully self-confident. Already sure I have found my teacher; I leave the hall wondering when I might listen to more Vedanta. Just outside the door is a table with books, pamphlets, and some literature about the ashram in Saylorsburg. A brochure gives the ashram's name as *Arsha Vidya Gurukulam* or A.V.G. I read that *arsha* means "of the rishis," the ancient wise men who first received and preserved the Vedas. *Vidya* means "knowledge." *Gurukulam* means "the teacher's home," where students go for instruction as they had done traditionally for hundreds of years in Vedic India.

I enroll in the first available class, scheduled for May 1988. I will attend as many retreats as my schedule allows me each year. Eventually, perhaps I will gain some real understanding of third-plateau spiritual development.

CHAPTER 10:

Western Mystics and Eastern Wise Men: Stages of Spiritual Growth

Since my first introduction to the Saylorsburg ashram, I continue studying there for at least two weeks a year, and, many years, I attend the Christmas week camp as well. In daily contact with Swami Dayananda—in lectures, in small group talks or *satsangs*, and in a dozen or so private interviews for this book—it does not take long to confirm that he is, indeed, a fully enlightened being. I also come to know five other ultimately matured people whom Swami Dayananda has taught. Two of these five are swamis with their own ashrams in India. Each teaches at Saylorsburg a few months a year while Swami Dayananda is elsewhere. A third swami has an ashram in the U.S. where he works full-time. Two are instructors who choose to remain in family life to model an enlightened lifestyle for Western householders. Each one is as impressive as the next. Close interaction with them teaches me far more than words can tell. Having described my Piagetian developmental scale as applied to first- and second-plateau individuals in Parts One and Two, and finally having come to know these third-plateau men and women, I feel ready to write about growth from Autonomy to Enlightenment or, as Swami Dayananda calls it, Ultimate mental health.

In the ancient Vedic culture of at least 3000 years ago, enlightenment was routinely taught in school, and society was underpinned by spiritual cohesion. Young boys, at twelve years old, go to a guru's home for intensive study of Sanskrit and the Vedas. They return twelve years later as young adults, already steeped in Vedanta and ready to begin life as householders. Young women had their own course of study in Vedic knowledge. The central teaching to these young people was that the reality of the whole manifestation is Unity Consciousness, in which all things, sentient and insentient are One. This makes one's neighbor as oneself and promotes compassionate love instead of the jealousy and competitive enmity that Western youth learn in a materialistic society, which has lost its grounding in spirituality. After marrying, raising their children, and finishing the business of worldly life, mature Vedic parents bequeath their worldly goods to their chlidren and go into retirement. They become *vanaprasthah* (forest dwellers), living simple lives, devoting their time to study and prehaps pursuing enlightenment. This life pattern still survives as the ideal in Vedic India.

As we shall see, during the middle ages, in the West, the journey toward enlightenent could be—as it remains today—a terrifying and painful process, requiring as it does the destruction of the personal, oppositional ("thinking" vs "working"), ego. It entails the extinction of "me and my story." Vedic Indians understand that such "loss" is really gain, since it is the troublesome "thinking" ego that creates the illusion of an isolated individual in a separate body. They know that its demise leads directly to merger with the source and that they will retain a functional or working ego to orient, organize, and stabilize them as they live out the remainder of their lives on earth.

The mystics will show us that even in their harsh and restritive cultures, angst can be reduced by successful examples of survivors of the stormy passage; but, throughout the ages, only in India has a traditional culture advocating enlightenment as life's goal survived. Even today, in India, *sadhus* like Swami Brahmananda from Chapter 8 tread familiar ground with active role models and a wealth of teachers available to guide their search for divine union or *Moksha*. Young men and women still study Vedic literature and Sanskrit and revere their ancestral traditions.

The ancient Vedantins sometimes used the metaphor of a red-hot iron ball to symbolize the relationship of consciousness to the human mind. The glowing red heat and the hard round metal appear as a single entity, just as consciousness and the mind are taken to be one. In reality, the hot iron is a composite of fire and metal, seen as one through superimposition of the two elements upon each other. In its finely honed teaching methodology, Vedanta uses this as one metaphor to clarify that the mind derives its consciousness as a *reflection* of the unity consciousness in which it shines and *not* because it generates consciousness within itself. Though this notion of the isolated self in a separate body with a discrete awareness of its own is deeply ingrained in each of us through millennia of body-identification, it is *false*. The only true source of conscious-

Third Plateau

Adolescence			Youth		Maturity
Adolescent Phase			Youth and Maturity		
Identity vs. Role Diffusion			Intimacy vs. Isolation	Generativity vs. Stagnation	Ego Integrity vs. Despair
Representational Period					
Stage XI	Stage XII	Stage XIII	Stage XIV	Stage XV	Stage XVI
Subceptions: Bare Grasp of Concepts	Bare Grasp of Concepts (continued)	Reflexive Behavioral Grasp of Concepts Without Ability to Verbalize Activity	Behavioral Grasp of Concepts Without Ability to Verbalize Activity	Reflective Abstractions Behavioral and Verbal Grasp of Concepts and Actions	Abstract Thought With Hypothetical and Deductive Reasoning
Stage XI	Stage XII	Stage XIII	Stage XIV	Stage XV	Stage XVI
Integration/Fusion	Eclipsing	Splitting	Twinning	Shuttling	Integration
Autonomy/Adolescence	Purification	illumination	Active or Resistant Dark Night of the Soul	Passive or Compliant Dark Night of the Soul	Enlightenment
none	none	none	none	none	none
Vedic studies continue sravanam/mananam/nididhyasanam			family and community life, children		Retirement, Advanced spritual study/Renunciation/Moksah
Conversion	Purification	illumination	Dark Night of the Soul		Unitive Way

Various Theorists Developmental Timetable

First Plateau

Theorists	0–4 weeks	1–4 Months	4–8 Months	8–12 Months	12–18 Months
Sigmund Freud		Early Oral Sucking Phase	Late Oral Sadistic Phase	Late Oral Sadistic Phase	Early Anal Phase
Rene Spitz	Normal Autistism — 0 to 3 months "Objectless State" of Non-differentiation	Normal Autistism — 0 to 3 months "Objectless State" of Non-differentiation	3 to 8 months "Precursor to the Object" 8-month Smile Begins Object Relations	8 to 15 months Stage of Libidinal Object 15 month "No" Response Begins Autonomous Self	8 to 15 months Stage of Libidinal Object 15 month "No" Response Begins Autonomous Self
Margret Mahler *(Normal Autism + Symbiosis / Separation)*	Autism	Symbiosis	1st Subphase of Differentiation "Hatching" Height of Separation Anxiety (8 months)	2nd Practicing Subphase, Early Begin Upright Posture + Bond to Mo. (7 to 8 months)	2nd Practicing Subphase Proper "love affair with world" (10/12 to 16/18 months)
Erik Erikson	Trust vs. Mistrust	Trust vs. Mistrust	Trust vs. Mistrust	Trust vs. Mistrust	Autonomy vs. Doubt and Shame
Jean Piaget *(Sensorimotor Period)*	Stage I — Use of Reflexes	Stage II — 1st Acquired Adaptations (Habits)	Stage III — Secondary Circular Reactions (Making Interesting Sights Last)	Stage IV — Coordination of Schemes to New Situations (Invention)	Stage V — Tertiary Reactions or Discovery of New Means
Catherine Morrison Stage	Stage I	Stage II	Stage III	Stage IV	Stage V
Stage Signature	Fusion	Eclipsing	Splitting	Twinning	Shutting
Normal Development	Autism	Normal Narcissism	Normal Narcissism	Normal Symbiosis	Normal Symbiosis
The Pathology of Developmental Delay	Psychosis	Narcissistic Character	Borderline Personality	Symbiotic or Primitive Neurotic Personality	Symbiotic Personality or Symbiotic Neurotic
Vedas					
Evelyn Underhill					

Second Plateau

Theorists	18-24 Months	2-4 Years	4-7 Years	7-9 Years	9-11 Years
Sigmund Freud	Late Anal Sadistic Phase	Early Oedipal Phase	Late Oedipal Phase	Latency Phase	Latency Phase
Rene Spitz					
Margret Mahler *(Individuation)*	3rd Subphase "Rapprochement" Upright Posture + Refueling Behavior (15 to 24 months)	4th Subphase Consolidation of Individuality + Beginning of Object Constancy	4 Year Old Identity Established and Object Constancy Continues to Solidify		
Erik Erikson	Autonomy vs. Doubt and Shame	Initiative vs. Guilt		Industry vs. Inferiority	
Jean Piaget	Sensorimotor Period — Stage VI — Inventions of New Means by Mental Combination	Representational Period — Preconcepts	Simple and Articulated Intuitions	Initial Concrete Subperiod	Mature Concrete Subperiod
Catherine Morrison Stage	Stage VI	Stage VII	Stage VIII	Stage IX	Stage X
Stage Signature	Integration/Fusion	Eclipsing	Splitting	Twinning	Shuttling
Normal Development	Beginning Personality Formation	Passive Egocentric or "Anal" Phase	Active Egocentric or "Phallic" Phase	"Genital" Phase (Latency)	"Oedipal" Integration Phase (Latency)
The Pathology of Developmental Delay	"Oral" or Compliant Personality	"Anal" or Oppositional Personality	"Phallic" or Oedipal Conflictual Personality	"Genital" or Oedipal Resolved Personality	Integrated Neurotic Personality
Vedas		start teaching alphabet	spiritual training + teaching music		
Evelyn Underhill					

ness is *atma* or *Brahman*, The One-Without-A-Second. Vedanta teaches that this source of all, being non-dual, is the source of consciousness that reflects in the otherwise insentient cellular matter constituting our bodies as well as our brains. This phenomenon is compared with sunlight shining on the surface of a lake or a mirror, making it bright by reflecting in it.

How does an essentially insentient brain, enlivened by reflected consciousness—but embattled with a self-centered ego that intuits progress along this third plateau will bring about its destruction—ever make the leap from that 'ego-mind,' even from a *"prepared* ego-mind," to identify with pure consciousness and become enlightened? What is the progression along the third plateau? Our society seems to have lost the inspiration and the motivation as well as the map. We can look for some of all three in this chapter. The mystics are good map-makers of their personal routes toward the Unitive Life, while the Vedantins' perfected teaching methodology shortens the quest and substantially diminishes its overwhelming anxiety. Diminished anxiety alone increases one's capacity for receptivity to Vedanta's message. We can benefit from the mystics and from others who record their paths toward enlightenment, and we can learn from today's Vedantins whose well-systematized teaching methods still beckon seekers from around the world. Perhaps these models can reignite our interest and inspire us toward our own maturational and spiritual progress, and I feel certain they can help us find our way.

Evelyn Underhill's classic *Mysticism* is an important source of information about Western aspirants. She studied and cataloged the lives of nearly a hundred individuals as they sought union with God. She identifies five stages, three for preparation and two for fruition. She calls her first stage "Conversion" or "Awakening of the Self." By Conversion, Underhill does not mean the novice or agnostic's first introduction to the notion of God. Instead, she refers to a deep, often sudden, shift in one's perception of reality, like that of St. Paul on the road to Damascus. In this Conversion, the self profoundly intuits that 1) God is real, 2) the world is a mock reality, and 3) the self is one with divinity. My own Conversion experience, though far less dramatic than St. Paul's, had the potency of a blow to the head, leaving me dazed. It accompanied the first complete Vedanta instruction I received from Swami Dayananda at the MIT lecture, reorienting my thought and galvanizing my passion toward the single goal of God-consciousness.

Reading and studying the spiritual experience of others has been highly instructive and compelling for me. The same is reported by Western aspirants centuries ago, and I think it will also prove true for today's readers. Therefore, I have taken great pains to cull and to quote the mystics and wise men whose own words speak powerfully *for* them and *to* us, as they describe the journey's progress.

First stage Conversion is a Piagetian fusion stage. Therefore, it lacks conflict, and shows the seeker a gloriously transfigured world filled with the presence of a loving God. "Ecstatic fusion" comes with this first intimation of unity consciousness. Coventry Patmore says the awakened soul realizes, "God is the only Reality, and we are real only as far as we are in His order and He is in us."(1) Here, however, one's fusion still includes the self-centered ego, which must be eliminated on this plateau.

Conversion can manifest as God's divine presence in the everyday world. St. Teresa of Avila, already a nun, with her life dedicated to God, reports,

> "In the beginning it happened to me that I was ignorant of one thing—I did not know that God was in all things: and when He seemed to me to be so near, I thought it impossible. [Yet] not to believe that He was present was not in my power; for [His presence] seemed...evident." When told thereafter by "...unlearned men..." that God was in Heaven and appeared in the world only by grace, "...I could not believe that, because, He seemed [so] present Himself: [that] I was distressed." [St. Teresa's spiritual mentor, St. John of the Cross, soon validated her Conversion experience and restored her to the joy of God's presence] "in all things." (2)

When she begins to chronicle her evolution toward enlightenment in 1941, Etty Hillesum is a twenty-seven-year-old Jewish woman living in Nazi-occupied Holland. Early in her diary, she records an emotionally charged experience that brings her into Conversion. Relieving some chronic physical symptoms, this experience ends her need to possess beautiful things, especially people and their preferential feelings for her. She writes that her:

> "grasping attitude...suddenly fell away....
> A thousand tyrannical chains were broken
> and I breathed freely again and felt strong
> and looked about with shining eyes. And
> now that I don't want to own anything any
> more and am free, now I suddenly own
> everything, now my inner riches are im-
> measurable." (3)

Underhill's second stage is the "Purification of the Self," that the mystics sometimes call "purgation." (4) Here the initial joyous revelation of a God-infused universe alternates sharply with the contrasting view of one's own shortcomings. The parallel stage on the first plateau is the Narcissistic Personality, in which the individual demands grandiose mirroring by the world or idealizes others and depreciates himself. In this all-or-nothing, eclipse stage on the third plateau, spiritual development juxtaposes the world of Conversion filled with God against the seeker's deep sense of unworthiness. Here, if the individual aggrandizes himself above God, he is a powerful personality, very often an infamous, psychopathic one.

During Purification, St. Catherine of Siena hears her spiritual voice say, "If thou wilt arrive at a perfect knowledge and enjoyment of Me, the Eternal Truth.... In self knowledge, then, thou wilt humble thyself, seeing that, in thyself, thou dost not even exist."(5) The unhappy seeker's task is to cleanse herself, in the hope that she may one day be worthy of union with the divine.

During her all-or-nothing purgation phase, Etty Hillesum says, "There is a really deep well inside me. And in it dwells God. Sometimes I am there too. But, more often stones and grit block the well, and God is buried beneath. Then He must be dug out again."(6) Cleansing herself, the unhappy seeker labors to re-enter and remain in God's mirroring presence.

In her purgation, St. Catherine of Genoa likens the soul to

> "...a covered object, the object cannot respond to the rays of the sun, not because the sun ceases to shine—for it shines without intermission—but because the covering intervenes.... Thus the souls are covered by a rust—that is, by sin—which is gradually consumed away by the fire of purgatory. The more it is consumed, the more they respond to God, their true Sun."(7)

"The essence of purgation," says Richard of St. Victor, "is self-simplification." (8) Henry David Thoreau's message throughout *Walden* is, "Simplicity, simplicity, simplicity!" (9) Vedanta also counsels simplification, expunging self-love and worldly interests in an attitude of dispassion and discrimination.

My personal experience of Stage XII occurs over a several-year period as the profundity of the meaning of Vedanta's teachings become more deeply ingrained through repeated exposure to them at the Saylorsburg ashram. I come away from these two or three weeks each year with a gradually increased clarity about my goal and an equally clear understanding that I am far from attaining it. I also recognize an ever-growing and seemingly insatiable desire for this spiritual knowledge.

At Purification, many mystics go into their own "therapy," imposing "spiritual austerities" on themselves, sometimes figurative and sometimes literal self-torturous attempts to annihilate the self-centered ego, which is seen to hamper progress. These distorted attempts at purgation can be egregious. Heinrich Suso, a fourteenth-century Dominican, spends sixteen years torturing himself with irons, nails, and hair shirts. Finally, a voice speaks to him saying, "It is enough," and immediately he throws his instruments of torture into a nearby river. (10)

Others suffer in emotional ways, but all look with loathing upon the physical body or the psychological trait that they see as separating them from God. St. Teresa is a very social person, whose friends come to her convent to talk with her at the grated opening in the wall. Though never chastised for this indulgence, Teresa feels these pleasures a deterrent to her spiritual advancement and eventually refuses the treats. (11)

Both St. Teresa and St. Francis of Assisi feel earthly beauty brings them closer to the Divine but think such pleasure selfish and an interference with spiritual growth. Each aspirant searches his own soul for impediments. St. John of the Cross says, "Desires and attachments affect the soul as the remora is said to affect a ship; that is but a little fish, yet when it clings to the vessel it effectively hinders its progress." (12)

Underhill's third and final preparation stage is called "Illumination" and is marked by an ecstatic vision of the Divine and an elevated feeling of union with God. Illumination bears a similarity to Conversion, but divine connection has deepened through the work done during purgation, and it continues to increase throughout Illumination. Even so, at this third stage, the oscillation of conflicting pairs of opposites create either/or splitting. Rulman Merswin says, "God shows Himself by turns harsh and gentle: to each access of misery succeeded the rapture of supernatural grace."(13)

The third-phase conflict is between a purified self, increasingly divested of worldly attachments and a greatly sanctified and lucid vision of God as universal essence. Stripped of grosser features, lenses cleared of "dust" for perceiving divinity, now the seeker's task is similar to, but subtler than before. At Illumination, he discards attachments and gathers strength for the next stage in which his relationship to God will become more complex. At its apex, however, third-stage joy brings so heightened an awareness of God's presence that the Jesuit poet Gerard Manley Hopkins can write,

> "The World is charged with the grandeur
> of God: It will flame out, shining like
> shook foil; It gathers to a greatness, like
> the ooze of oil Crushed…."

and,

> "I caught this morning morning's minion,
> kingdom of daylight's dauphin, dapple-
> dawn-drawn Falcon, in his riding...."
> Rebuffed the big wind. My heart in hiding
> Stirred for a bird,—the achieve of; the
> mastery of the thing!
> Brute beauty and valour and act, oh, air,
> pride, plume, here
> Buckle! AND the fire that breaks from
> thee then, a billion
> Times told lovelier, more dangerous, O
> my chevalier!
> No wonder of it: sheer plod makes plough
> down sillion
> Shine, and blue-bleak embers, ah my dear,
> Fall, gall themselves, and gash gold-ver-
> million. (14)

Jacob Boehme says of Illumination,

> "Now was I come up in spirit through the
> flaming sword into the Paradise of God....
> The creation was opened to me; and it was
> showed me how all things had their names
> given them, according to their nature and
> virtue...as people come into subjection to
> the Spirit of God, and grow up in the im-
> age and power of the Almighty, they may
> receive the *hidden unity* in the *Eternal Be-*

ing." (15)

At Illumination, Etty Hillesum feels that loving and caring about individual lives is selfish. Only loving humanity and life itself matters. Despite her unusual circumstances, she can say, "I have gradually come to realize that on those days when you are at odds with your neighbors you are really at odds with yourself." She concentrates on broadening and deepening her "inner well" of God, keeping any personal or egoistic feelings, the "sand and grit," from impeding "the great stream of life that flows through the divine well" within every human being. Though acutely embarrassed by a deeply intimate act, inconsistent with her own Jewish tradition, she describes herself as a "kneeler in training" and is occasionally stunned to find herself on her knees in prayer "almost automatically. Forced to the ground by something stronger than myself." (16)

The first fruition stage is Stage XIV, the surrender of one's self to God. It is called the "Dark Night of the Soul." Fourth-position stages on all plateaus are dramatic. It is here that the both/and drive design replaces third position alternation between either/or. At each stage of development there is ambivalence about giving up the known in order to advance and gain self-knowledge, but the pull in both directions reaches its peak at the fourth stage, especially on the third plateau. Stage XIV presents a clear watershed. One senses that in going forward there is no turning back. Nearing the steep peak of the developmental hill and pushing hard toward the top means reaching the crest where momentum down the other side gives progress a life of its own.

The severity of the emotional cost of progress on the third plateau is new. Previous attempts to unify conflicted self-concepts at every stage—however painful—always left the seeker a personal foundation. Until now, out of every integration comes a broader psychological entity that includes a more definitive ego and a healthier egoistic self. One's old familiar and separate personal identity not only remains intact but feels more solid. On this final plateau, the ego actually weakens with each stage, but even so the loving embrace of God makes the seeker feel stronger and more secure. Now, however, at Stage XIV, it becomes painfully clear that the cost of continuing to seek a closer relationship with the absolute is individual psychological identity itself. No self can be salvaged from this quest. Here is the point of no return, for the seeker now realizes all he has left of a self is the subtlest ghost of an autonomous egoistic I-sense, and he knows that this too must now be discarded if he is to proceed.

The new vision of an impersonal self takes some getting used to. Grieving the loss of the last vestige of this ego is a significant part of the emotional work of the fourth position. Troublemaker though it is, one has long been attached to being "special" by means of enhancing, refining, and preening—even purifying—the ego. Never before has development asked the seeker to abandon it altogether. Here the mystics say God abandons *them*, insisting—as with Abraham and Isaac—that the seeker sacrifice everything most dear to him: his heart, his soul, his will, his all.

In the metaphor of the red-hot iron ball, Vedanta

clarifies that the mind becomes conscious by reflecting consciousness and does not itself generate that consciousness. At Stage XIV, refinement and integration all but destroy what is left of the ego in the fire of consciousness. What were two but *appeared* as one now *become* as one in the both/and relationship. William Blake refers to this juncture as two "planes"—the "World of Becoming," tainted with the ego, and the "World of Being," belonging to the absolute. (17) But crossing the divide is terrifying, with a dying ego now behaving like a demon possessed as one of the both/and pairs and God-merger still invisible as the other, the aspirant feels doomed to the bottomless pit of hell.

Underhill thinks of Illumination as an important "resting" place for the consolidation of previous gains before conflict reemerges and pushes the seeker forward into the depths of this awesome final struggle. At the Dark Night stage, the seeker's both/and awareness illuminates his stark identity choice. Here the first impediment to enlightenment, which is psychological immaturity, gives way to the second impediment, the existential fear of personal extinction. Spiritual maturation has reached its crisis. Thus, at Illumination, more frequently than at any other third-plateau stage, many seekers—in their joyful relationship with the Divine and intuiting that fourth stage agony—abandon their pursuit of the "Unitive Life," settling into the considerable advances made and the rewards gained at third-stage Illumination.

The mystics clearly dread the third-plateau "divide" between the preparation and the completion phases on the path to God Consciousness. The divine voice of St.

Catherine of Sienna tells her that God never withdraws from those who are now one with Him in enlightenment but only from those whom He is "leading on to perfection." (18) This is the juncture Heinrich Suso notes between the Lower and the Upper Schools. St. John of the Cross calls Stage XIII "Bethlehem," a happy place, and compares it to the "Calvary" of Stage XIV which will follow. He says, "For the many that come to Bethlehem, there be few that will go on to Calvary" (19). It was St. John, himself, referring to "Calvary," who coined the phrase "Dark Night of the Soul."

At "resting" Stage XIII, the seeker is immersed in the vision of the world unified by God and is deeply conscious of the life he shares with all creation. However, the greater the longing and capacity of the seeker, the sooner he will realize, with fourteenth-century German mystic Johann Tauler, that he is not yet at his ultimate goal. Tauler says, "The heavenly Manna which has been administered to him is not yet that with which the angels are full fed... and hence there remains an eternal hunger and impatience. If God gave to such a man all the gifts which all the saints possess, and all that He is able to give, but without giving Himself, the craving desire of the spirit would remain hungry and unsatisfied." (20)

In her fruition phase of mystical development, Underhill categorizes two, not three, stages. One is her very long, foreboding fourth stage which she calls by St. John's title: "The Dark Night of the Soul." Her fifth and final stage is the "Unitive Life," enlightenment or *Moksha*. As I read the lives of the mystics, however, I distinguish two aspects of their Dark Night. My study differentiates a Piagetian fourth and fifth stages incorporated in Underhill's long fourth—a first *actively* resistant phase (Stage XIV), followed by a second *passively* submissive Stage XV. In the fifth position of Piaget's rapid shuttling stage, conflicting urges begin to quiet and to quell the Dark Night conflict. At this fifth position, the mortally wounded ego ceases its struggle. With this shift, the seeker's alienation from the absolute feels less acute, and Dark Night is lit by the dawn of new hope. The final death of the personal ego at Stage XVI is, indeed, the Dark Night's integration, and this achievement leaves a "void" already filled by God— the Piagetian sixth or completion stage—enlightenment, the Unitive Life, or *Moksha*. We will see this fifth stage as our examples struggle through it.

Although he describes his experience in psychological and philosophical terms rather than in the personal and religious language of the mystics, Carl Jung provides a poignant example of the Dark Night's first phase: its active resistant mode and perhaps even the accompanying fear of personal extinction which infused many of the mystics at this juncture. Having vigorously pursued man's relationship to God all his life, Jung gains sufficient sophistication to enter Stage XIV. Rising above the fourth-stage clouds, he catches a glimpse of his goal. In comparing his second-plateau fourth-stage turmoil, with his present state of emotional evolution, Jung writes:

> What, on a lower level, had led to the wildest conflicts and to panicky outbursts of

emotion, from the higher level of personality now looked like a storm in the valley seen from the mountain top. This does not mean that the storm is robbed of its reality, but instead of being in it one is above it. But since, in a psychic sense, we are both valley and mountain, it might seem a vain illusion to deem oneself beyond what is human. One certainly does feel the effect and is shaken and tormented by it, yet at the same time one is aware of a higher consciousness looking on which prevents one from becoming identical with the affect, a consciousness which regards the affect as an object, and can say, "I know that I suffer." What our text says of indolence, "Indolence of which man is conscious, and indolence of which he is unconscious, are a thousand miles apart," holds true in the highest degree of affect. (21)

Jung studies Eastern religions, believing their message holds valuable insights for Western spiritual growth. He clearly sees the difference that a more mature perspective affords, but he is so embedded in his own formulations of ego and of consciousness, in Western psychology and its dualistic underpinnings, that he rejects his insights. In her in-depth study of Jung and Vedanta, Dr. Carol Whitfield tells us that, for Jung, consciousness is created by the accumulation of knowledge which the ego gathers as it matures.

Consciousness is thus produced by subject/object duality, and must, of course, retain this dual character, making it incompatible with Vedanta's essential principle of unity. She adds that Jung did not explore the subject's nature, his essential being, which Vedanta knows as "pure consciousness," but discarded this as "empty" or "useless," never appreciating the self-luminous, "being-knowing-limitless" background, the "presence" of all things, which Vedanta shows it to be. (see page XX).

Soon Jung is arguing that Westerners must not utilize Eastern concepts, directly, but must first earn the right to do so. He says:

> By an inevitable decree of fate the West is becoming acquainted with the peculiar facts of Eastern spirituality. It is useless either to belittle these facts, or to build false and treacherous bridges over yawning gaps.... If we snatch these things directly from the East, we have merely indulged our Western acquisitiveness, confirming yet again that 'everything good is outside,' whence it has to be fetched and pumped into our barren souls.... The philosophy of the East, although so vastly different from ours, could be an inestimable treasure for us too; but in order to possess it, we must first earn it. (22)

Jung, as our "Vedic antagonist," continues expounding his conclusions stating that enlightenment is impossible for a Westerner to achieve without much psychological integration of his Self-image and much philosophical integration of the Western God-image. He continues expressing his conclusions by saying only an Easterner may achieve enlightenment. Renouncing his Eastern insights into a deeper, more inclusive understanding of God-consciousness, Jung says, "The Eastern mind, however, has no difficulty in conceiving of a consciousness without an ego. Consciousness is deemed capable of transcending its ego condition; indeed, in its "higher" forms, the ego disappears altogether. Such an egoless mental condition can only be unconsciousness to us, for the simple reason that there would be nobody to witness it." (23)

Sadly, especially as he had come so far in his development, Jung now draws the conclusion that only an Eastern thinker with his "quick knowing realization(s)," can become enlightened. Then, he goes so far as to deny the possibility of enlightenment to an Easterner as well, saying:

> One cannot know something that is not distinct from oneself. Even when I say "I know myself," an infinitesimal ego—the knowing "I"—is still distinct from "myself" in this as it were atomic ego, which is completely ignored by the essentially non-dualist standpoint of the East, there nevertheless lies hidden the whole unembellished pluralistic universe and its unconquered reality. The experience of

the "at-one-ment" is one example of the
"quick knowing" realizations of the East,
as intuition of what it would be like if
one could exist and not exist at the same
time.... But for my part I cannot conceive
of such a possibility. I therefore assume
that in this point, Eastern intuition has
overreached itself. (24)

Vedanta says that Jung, standing at the very thresh-
old of his much-coveted search for ultimate union with
God, fails to realize the goal he seeks because he has no
qualified teacher to instruct him. In fact, that atomic ego, his
knowing "I," *is* distinct from his true Self; but its absence
is not self-annihilating as he concludes. Seeing himself and
his thoughts of self-knowledge, *does*, mean he cannot *be*
those thoughts or that *I-knower*. From the second plateau,
we know that thoughts are as much objects to the subject as
is the physical body. Jung's problem is that, after his own
"quick knowing" realization of higher consciousness, he rejects it and essentially returns to his old constricted view.

However, Jung could not have observed his own
"higher consciousness looking on," preventing confusion
of self with object, without being aware of that higher consciousness. Thus, initially correctly seeing, Jung becomes
– perhaps fearful—but certainly confused by his limited understanding of "ego" and of "consciousness." He backs away
from his own critical insight, and draws a false conclusion.
Properly discriminated, consciousness belongs only to the
Self or *atma*. All else, including a *thought* of the Self as the

knowing "I," are objects to the Self and are dependent upon it for their being. So the conceptual "I" thought *doesn't* really exist, as Jung understands and states, but his initial intuition of the "higher intelligence looking on," *does* exist, and is, in fact, the ever present, all-seeing, itself unseen, Witness Consciousness or *saksi*. Realization that one is and has always been this Witness Consciousness, this *saksi*--and never the body/mind/sense complex—makes letting go the conceptual "I" thought a relief and not a terror.

Jung's dilemma and that of many mystics who struggle and falter—sometimes fatally as Jung does, other times only arduously and tortuously as Suso does—illustrate the value of a spiritual teaching methodology. Many religions and philosophies espouse the essence of the upanishadic vision, but none of them provides the clear explanatory message or the systematic teaching method that is the heart of Vedanta. Swami Dayananda explains this carefully in Chapter 9: all mithya objects, including thoughts, can be taken apart and/or negated, while only *satyam* or consciousness (The-One-Without-A-Second) is reality.

For all their attempts to codify their experiences, the Christian mystics do not offer a systematic method. Though their developmental stages overlap and coincide, each mystic follows his or her own personal path in arriving at similar positions and insights as they journey toward the Unitive Life. Discerning the similarities of their paths to the goal is left to the biographer, like Underhill, and, if one does not understand where one is along the way, or why it is one feels despair and terror—if there is no map to guide one—then progress can become painful and difficult indeed.

Of the Dark Night, Meister Eckhart says that God "acts as if there were a wall erected between Him and us." (25) And St. John of the Cross, using his own italics for emphasis, writes that here God "abandoned (the soul), *of which it has no doubt*; that He has cast it away into darkness as an abominable thing…. All this and even more the soul feels now, for a terrible apprehension has come upon it that thus it will be for ever. It has also the same sense of abandonment with respect to all creatures, and that it is an object of contempt to all, especially to its friends." (26)

In the active, resistant Dark Night, not only God, but the world too, seem to turn against the hapless seeker. Everything, both spiritual and practical, goes wrong. Madame Guyon, an eighteenth-century French woman who catalogues every nuance of feeling along her spiritual journey, writes, "It is an amazing thing for a soul that believed herself to be advanced in the way of perfection, when she sees herself thus go to pieces all at once." (27)

During this phase of Etty Hillesum's development, her external world has spun out of control. Nazi intentions to exterminate the Jews are becoming undeniably clear. Deprived of their jobs and professions, Amsterdam's Jews are being forced to wear the Star of David, to live in ghettos, and some are being collected at Westerbork, a transit camp near the German border. From there they will be sent, systematically, in weekly trainloads, to extermination camps in Germany, Poland, and elsewhere. Etty writes, "Dante's Inferno is comic opera by comparison" to what the Jews suffer at the hands of the Nazis. "Ours is the real Hell." (28)

While many mystic seekers abandon their journey

at Illumination for fear of self-extinction, others turn more fervently to their own inner voices or to a more advanced and wiser spiritual guide and continue the quest. St. Teresa of Avila turns to St. John of the Cross, who has suffered mightily during his Dark Night experience. He not only comforts and reassures her but works with her to reform the Carmalite Order.

Of the acceptance stage of the Dark Night, Lucie-Christine, a nineteenth-century French mystic, says, "At the end of such a long and cruel transition, how much more supple the soul feels itself to be in the Hand of God, how much more detached from all that is not God! She sees clearly in herself the fruits of humility and patience, and feels her love ascending more purely and directly to God in proportion as she has realized the Nothingness of herself and all things." (29)

If the seeker wishes to pursue his goal and proceed to The Unitive Life, the *task* of this fourth resistant stage (XIV) is the infliction of the ego with a mortal wound in preparation for its final surrender to, or melding with, the will of God. We shall see a supremely successful example of this in Etty, despite her brutal circumstances. Toward the end of the Dark Night, in its passive phase, the ego ceases its struggle with the "Almighty Order." It rails less fiercely, and begins to accept its fate. Passage through its active struggle leads to the passive phase of Dark Night surrender (XV).

When Etty is coming to terms with her plight, she says, "[and] I have not been entirely honest with myself. I shall have to learn this lesson, too, and it will be the most difficult of all, oh God, to bear the suffering you have imposed on me and not just the suffering I have chosen for myself." (30) Because she feels she can help more in Westerbork than in Amsterdam, Etty volunteers to go there with the first group of Jews sent.

During her acceptance phase, as she prepares to go to Westerbork, Etty writes, "If you have a rich inner life, there probably is not that much difference between the inside and outside of a camp. Would I myself be able to live up to such sentiments? There are few illusions left to us. Life is going to be very hard. We shall be torn apart, all who are dear to one another, I don't think the time is very far off now."

Only a few weeks later, on a short leave from the camp, she confirms the strength of her inner union with God, Stage XVI, and puts to rest her suspicions that her external surroundings can destroy it. It is clear from this passage that Eddy already intuits the highest truth: while individual lives may end, *life* itself is the manifestation. In God's hands and control, it can never be destroyed by human activity of any kind. In fact, that activity itself is part of the manifestation, for nothing is *outside* it. Affirming her deep understanding of this profound wisdom, she writes:

> "I know the persecution and oppression and despotism and the impotent fury and the terrible sadism. I know it all. And yet at unguarded moments, when left to myself, I suddenly lie against the naked breast of life and her arms round me are so gentle and so protective and my own heartbeat is difficult

to describe: so slow and so regular and so
soft, almost muffled, but so constant, as if
it would never stop. That is my attitude to
life and I believe that neither wars nor any
other senseless human atrocity will ever be
able to change it." (31)

In their deepest contemplations, most mystics hear
or see an inner voice or vision that they identify as emanat-
ing directly from God. As each has a personal path, each
has his or her own name for the divine source of their intui-
tive knowledge. Plotinus calls it the "One," Eckhart and St.
John of the Cross call their voices the "All." Ruysbroeck's
name for his divine intuition is the "Unplumbed Abyss."
St. Catherine of Genoa calls her voice "Pure Love." Suso
calls his the "Eternal Wisdom."

Heinrich Suso, the fourteenth-century German
mystic quoted previously provides a crystalline, human,
and personally detailed account of the mystic's Dark Night
in its active and passive phases. Suso's Eternal Wisdom
speaks to him in symbolic visions. Many years after becoming a monk, in an early vision, he is bathed in a divine
light, relieving him of a lifelong restless nature. From ages
eighteen to forty, Suso practices his torturous austerities
until the Eternal Wisdom tells him, "Thou hast been long
enough in the Lower School, and hast there sufficiently applied thyself. Come, then with me: and I will introduce thee
into the highest school that exists in this world. There, thou
shalt apply thyself to the study of that science which will
procure thee the veritable peace of God; and which will

bring thy holy beginning to a happy end." (32)

Then Suso is introduced to the master of this highest school, who says to the assemblage, "Know that this guest is able to become a good disciple of our high science, if he will bear with patience the hard probation: for it is necessary that he be tried inwardly…. In this Upper School they teach the science of Perfect Self Abandonment; that is to say, that a man is here taught to renounce himself so utterly that, in all those circumstances in which God is manifested, either by Himself or in His creatures, the man applies himself only to remaining calm and unmoved, renouncing so far as is possible all human frailty." (33)

Following this vision, Suso examines himself inwardly and, speaking to himself in the second person, concludes he is still of:

> much self-will…and with all thy mortifications which thou hast inflicted on thyself, thou canst not yet endure external vexations." [He likenes himself to a] "hare hiding in a bush, who is frightened by the whispering of the leaves. Thou also art frightened every day by the griefs that come to thee: thou dost turn pale at the sight of those who speak against thee: when thou oughtest to present thyself with simplicity, thou dost hide thyself. When they praise thee, thou art happy: when they blame thee, thou art sad. Truly is it very needful for thee that Thou shouldst

go to an Upper School." (34)

When Suso asks the Eternal Wisdom what the lessons are that he must endure, he is told it is better not to know details, but that first his reputation will be ruined by powerful strangers and he will become an "object of contempt to blinded men." Second, he will lose his loving disposition and become greatly depressed, with nothing in his life but "unfaithfulness, great sufferings, and great griefs." Finally, "Hitherto thou hast been but a child at the breast, a spoiled child...immersed in the divine sweetness like a fish in the sea. Now, I will withdraw all this...[and] thou shouldst be abandoned of God and of man...[being without] 'consolation' [to endure suffering and] 'vexation.'" (35)

Suso's trials begin and continue for ten years. This quiet and timid man, as predicted, is forced to live in the world outside of monastic life, plagued with illness, physical hardship, and personal failure. A woman accuses Suso of being the father of her child, and the community believes the rumor and makes fun of Suso's "false" sanctity. Deeply crushed, Suso rails to God as Job had done. With the scandal at its height, another woman offers to destroy the child who will otherwise become Suso's financial responsibility and deeply damage his whole brotherhood. By now more humble and submissive, approaching Stage XV of acceptance, Suso gives a noble answer, saying, "I have confidence in the God of Heaven, Who is rich, and Who has given me until now all that which was needful to me.... Go fetch the little child that I may see it." When he holds the baby, Suso embraces it as well as all the trials God has sent.

With full passage into acceptance (XV), feeling great compassion for the orphaned child "cast off like a little dog," Suso says, "The providence of God hath given thee to me...and as long as heaven gives me a mouthful, I shall share it with thee, for the greater glory of God; and will patiently support all the trials that may come to me, my darling son!" (36) At last, abandoning himself fully to God's will, he says, "*fiat voluntas tua* [Thy will be done]," and his sense of ecstatic union with God returns. (37) Thus Suso enters the Unitive Life or *Moksha* and dwells in the knowledge of his identity with the absolute.

Swami Dayananda recounts a Dark Night experience from his Vedic path. As I have suggested, it is perhaps a function of Vedanta's clear teaching tradition with its guides and models, that his suffering is less prolonged and painful than that described by some of the mystics. Swami Dayananda's Dark Night comes several years after his decision to follow his guru, Swami Chinmayananda, and study Vedanta. By this time he has a good grasp of the subject matter, but several points trouble him. (38) One problem is the prevalent notion of Vedanta as a theory. Another is the companion notion that, to make the theory real one has to practice to gain the experience of *atma*, the witness consciousness. If Vedanta were a theory, he reasons, why is it any better than the other five or six theories arising from the Vedas? If experience has to prove it, then that experience, like all experiences, is subject to interpretation. Some people may feel genuine *atma* bliss while others might experience some other kind of bliss, narcissistic bliss, even "ice cream bliss," as he once joked. How could one ever know for sure that his or her experience was the real thing?

Thirdly, if *atma* or the witness consciousness is the experienced object, then the experiencer must be *anatma* or non-atma. The idea of such an experiencer, outside the whole and separate from it, destroys the essential idea of Vedanta as a nondual teaching. This is a *serious* set of flaws that severely trouble the swami. Though he cannot dismiss Vedanta, he begins to doubt the whole pursuit. He is thoroughly invested in this venture, but he has to admit that it might lead to a dead end.

Swami Dayananda cannot rest. There is no one to whom he can go with his questions because everyone he knows accepts and espouses the flaws he sees without being able to reconcile them. He casts about for answers. He investigates the teachings of Ramana Maharshi. He reads Krishnamurti, William Blake, William James, Ouspensky, Lao Tsu, and Zen philosophy. He is fascinated by the Christian mystics, by the immediacy of their language and by their experience of divine union. He continues to do his job as editor for Swami Chinmayananda while he searches for answers.

In this search, Swami Dayananda travels far and wide throughout India. Eventually he hears a talk by a man named Swami Pranavananda, who speaks Telugu. Swami Dayananda only partially understands Telugu, but he immediately intuits that this man knows something vital, and he makes arrangements to take a leave from his work to study with Swami Pranavananda at his ashram in Gudivada in central India.

Swami Pranavananda explains that Vedanta is neither a theory nor a philosophy. Instead, it is a means of knowledge, a *pramana*. As the eye is the valid means of knowledge for form and color, as the ear is for sound, so the whole of Vedanta's teaching method is the means for clarifying confusion as to the nature of reality and one's true identity. Vedanta is the direct means of knowledge, the *pramana*, for removing ignorance of *atma* as *Brahman*. "I," the witness consciousness, is always available for "experience." No one has to practice that to recognize it. It is always self-revealing, self-existent, non-negatable *satyam*, never *mithya*. Being that on which all else depends for existence, it is the only independent nonconceptual entity, "The One-Without-A-Second." It exists independent of proof. While there is no doubt that "I exist," people *do* doubt that "I" is *atma*. The doubts and confusions surrounding "I" as *atma* arise through misinterpreting *atma* by superimposition of the body/mind upon it. (This is the error that Jung makes when he assumes Easterners will become "unconscious," instead of enlightened, if they drop their conceptual "I" thought and rely on their higher consciousness for awareness.)

Swami Pranavananda explains that the whole teaching of Vedanta is to be used as a way of showing essential truth to the student. The student can understand the truth of himself immediately, while listening to the teaching, when that teaching is handled properly as a *pramana* by a qualified teacher. Swami Pranavananda says, "Neither a theory nor a philosophy, but a direct *pramana* for removing ignorance of *atma* as *Brahman*; that is the *Vedanta-Rahasyam*, the secret of Vedanta." Afterward, though he studies the *Brahma Sutra*

Basham with Swami Tarananda Giriji—which every serious swami must do—from the moment of his understanding Vedanta as *pramana*, Swami Dayananda's doubts vanish and, as he says, from that point on, "I never looked back."

Not all of Pujya Swamiji Dayananda's students are aware of this chapter in the life of the founder of our ashram. If Swami Dayananda had not been so astute and persistent, we could be learning a very different Vedanta, than the one we are so privileged to be learning today. For this contribution alone, we owe him an enormous debt of gratitude. It is a debt which we can never repay, but one which we should all know and profoundly appreciate.

With this knowledge, Swami Dayananda's Dark Night ends. Though bitter while it lasts, because of his own personal readiness and the ultimate availability of a clear teacher of clear teaching, Swami Dayananda passes through his Dark Night and is rather quickly relieved of his anguish.

Eckhart Tolle is another living master whose enlightenment, like that of Ramana Maharshi and some other masters, has enveloped him suddenly and as a whole. With little use for the past, he gives few details about it. Born in Germany in 1948, Tolle says his first thirteen years are "lived in a state of almost continuous anxiety interspersed with periods of suicidal depression." (39) Nevertheless, he manages to graduate from Cambridge University, where he becomes a research scholar and an advisor.

When he is twenty-nine years of age, one night Tolle has an enlightenment experience that sounds similar to, but even more profound, than that of St. Paul. He awakes with a terrible feeling of dread, more intense than ever before. Life feels alien, meaningless, and so loathsome that he finds no reason to live. He thinks he can "not continue to *live with*" *himself* and is suddenly struck by the implication of that statement. So, "Am I one person or am I two?" If he is two, maybe only *one* of these selves is real. He is so stunned by this realization that his mind stops, and he feels himself "sucked into a void," where there is no more fear and where life takes on fresh meaning, filled with a joy and a peace that never leave him. (40) Tolle spends the next several years absorbing and understanding what has happened to him and reading about various enlightenment traditions. Then, people begin to ask him to give them or show them how to get what he has, and he answers, "You have it already. You just can't feel it because your mind is making too much noise." (41) He has been teaching ever since.

At last, when one's mind is prepared and ready to go entirely beyond the initial Stages XII, XIII, and the final ego resolution of XIV and XV, to a positive realization of the self, one is ready to enter final Stage XVI. In her study of Jung and Vedanta mentioned earlier, Dr. Carol Whitfield (one of Swami Dayananda's ultimately matured students who lives and teaches as a private citizen) says that at this point one must turn the prepared mind toward the "subject, the conscious being." She says:

> If the mind which is turned toward the
> conscious Self, however, does not enjoy
> a condition which is similar to the Self,

then it is that condition which will be illumined and we will still have a subject/
object dichotomy. If, however, the mind
is similar in nature to the Self, it will be
overwhelmed or lost in the Self, similar
to a candle flame held up to the sun. The
mind, like the flame, becomes as though
invisible…offering no locus for objectifi-
cation which is other than consciousness
itself. It is in this condition that one experiences the nature of the Self not only as
consciousness and existence, but as infinite and full; in other words, free from any
sense of limitation. Even to use the word
"experience" here is misleading, because
there is no sensation of a subject/object
relationship attached to the experience.
Since the Self is self effulgent, its nature
is self-evident and does not need a second
knower to illumine it. Just as, for instance,
the sun does not need another sun to illumine it. (42)

At this completion phase, the yogic notion emerges
that one's very program for life is God-given, as are the results of one's activities. Without a personal agenda and with
the understanding that one's own will is God's will and that,
in fact, the identity of the seeker and the sought—the Self
and the Source—are One, the personal ego is fully resolved.
The witness consciousness is understood as *atma* or *Brah-*

man and ignorance is consumed in *Moksha*. Meister Eckhart says simply, "God is nearer to me than I am to myself, He is just as near to wood and stone, but they do not know it." (43)

Following his Job-like raving, against his bitter "Upper School lessons," Suso ends his personal autobiography with these words:

> And later when God judged that it was time, He rewarded the poor martyr for all his suffering. And he enjoyed peace of heart, and received in tranquility and quietness many precious graces. And he praised the Lord from the very depths of his soul, and thanked Him for those same sufferings: which, for all the world, he would not now have been spared. And God caused him to understand that by this complete abasement he had gained more, and was made the more worthy to be raised up to God, than by all the pains which he had suffered from his youth up to that time. (44)

In August 1943, a few days before she is transported to Auschwitz where a Red Cross report lists that she dies on November 30, 1943, Etty Hillesum writes:

> This afternoon I was resting on my bunk and suddenly I just had to write these few lines in my diary, and I now send them to

you: 'You have made me so rich, oh God, please let me share out Your beauty with open hands. My life has become an uninterrupted dialogue with You, oh God, one great dialogue. Sometimes when I stand in some corner of the camp, my feet planted on Your earth, my eyes raised towards Your Heaven, tears sometimes run down my face, tears of deep emotion and gratitude. At night, too, when I lie in my bed and rest in You, oh God, tears of gratitude run down my face, and that is my prayer. (45)

Simplicity, selflessness, and joyful application of energy to the task at hand characterize enlightened men and women. Knowing with Meister Eckhart that any work is God's work and that "His will is my will," they seem, again, like Swami Dayananda, with all doubts removed, to take up their work toward their enlightened goals tirelessly, humbly, and with utmost grace.

Enlightened mystics and swamis go quietly about their/God's business no matter how exalted or lowly that business may be. Suso continues to live quietly outside of his monastery, where he preaches and becomes a spiritual consultant to many. St. Francis always lives quietly, with extreme humility and in complete poverty, even after his fame has brought him many followers. He teaches and preaches to those who come to him. Catherine of Siena is both a nurse to the sick, a teacher to the poor, and a vigorous political force for reform in the Roman Catholic

Church. Catherine of Genoa founds the first hospital in her city of origin. This hospital becomes her home and the center of her Christian service. St. John of the Cross lives a life of varied duties. He is spiritual director to St. Teresa and the various homes for nuns that she establishes. He also builds buildings when necessary and once engineered a complex aqueduct system for conveying water to one of the convents. Together St. John and St. Theresa found the Discalced Carmelite Order. Ruysbroeck retires to a small community that he establishes under Augustinian rules in the forest of Soignes. There he lives quietly and writes many of his most profound works on mysticism.

Swami Dayananda is an eminent Vedanta teacher in the United States and in India. He has held talks and seminars in many other places around the world, including Europe, Australia, Hawaii, Singapore, etc. He has founded three ashrams, the third in Coimbatore in South India.

With his lifelong reputation for integrity and compassion, Swami Dayananda commands great respect in India and has been able to raise money and gather volunteers, workers, political assistance, and social help that ensure the success of a program he founded in the year 2000. This program, the All India Movement, or AIM, was first headed by R. Venandkatraman, a former president of India. Its mission statement is: "[to] bridge the gap between mainstream society and the less privileged people living in remote, rural, tribal, and urban areas of India by following a planned program of caring in terms of education, health care, women's empowerment and self-sufficiency, vocational training, environmental initiatives, disaster relief and cultural validation."

Headquarteded in New Delhi, by 2010, Aim has built 79 student homes or Chatralayas in fourteen states, twenty schools in five states serving more than 18,000 children, 100 Balwadis, or nursery schools, and more than 300 evening tuitorial centers for 8,000 children in India's 28 states. AIM has five hospitals in four states, six medical clinics in three states, and six mobile health units serving 5 states. These facilities touch 10,000,000 people in remote rural sites as well as in urban slums. In the branch offices of 11 Indian states, retired administrators have trained volunteers to manage internal affairs and bookkeeping, saving staff time for outreach work in the community. Most of the 593 districts in the country have been studied to assess existing needs and problems.

One branch of AIM, the Green India Campaign, has helped Indians plant well over 10,000 plants and trees. Another branch, called AIM for Sevya, focuses on Indian culture, crafts, and the preservation of ancient values, among the less-privileged people in all of India's remote sites, and city slums. AIM for Sevya serves women by giving them materials and support for reviving or continuing their traditional arts and crafts. They engage in such projects as block-printing patterns on cotton materials to make bedspreads and table cloths. They make jewelry, toys, and hand-stitched pashmina shawls. They also raise and weave cloth from *ahimsa* silk that is harvested in an ingenious way without killing the silk worms that spin the thread. These products are brought to worldwide markets, where they sell at fair market value, and the profits are returned to the communities that produced the goods. Swami Dayananda hopes that this program may serve as a model for other third-world countries that share the problems of threatened loss of native crafts, of employing village women, of getting saleable goods into city stores at fair prices, and of returning the profits earned to the communities that produced them, thus raising local standards of living. And, still, with responsibility for managing these enormous projects, Swami Dayananda continues to teach three months at Saylorsburg and to oversee a three year course in India.

Wherever these enlightened men and women go about their various duties and callings—in olden days as well as in modern times—they inevitably draw followers to themselves. No matter how quiet and unpretentious their lives, others recognize in them the profoundly special qualities of the Immutable, the Absolute, the Source, or *Isvara*. Swami Dayananda says, "The foremost of these qualities is compassion."

CHAPTER 11:

An End to "Beginningless" Ignorance

Having made the decision and prepared the way, I retire from psychotherapy practice in the fall of 2005. A few clients keep occasional phone contact, but for the first time since childhood, I am free of formal responsibility. Finally, I can participate in a longer study at *Arsha Vidya Gurukulam*. I join a three-month course, October to December, taught by Swami Tattvavidananda. The course material is the *Prasnopanisad*, with Sankaracarya's commentary, and the second chapter of the *Bhagavad Gita*. There are two *Prasna* classes in the morning, a *Gita* class in the evening, and *a satsang*—question-and-answer class—from 7:30 to 8:30 or 9:00.

Swami Tattvavidananda, who suggests we call him Swami TV, has taught at the Gurukulam for several years, but I have heard him only once during a two-week course held the previous year. I know he is an excellent teacher, with the unusual background of one PhD in chemistry and one in Sanskrit. I also know he is the son of a multigenerational family of Vedic scholars and that his father was his first teacher. Then he went on to join a traditional patashala for further Vedic and Sanskrit learning, and he completed his education with Swami Dayananda as his mentor.

During the retreat, I learn that Swami TV, an extraordinarily humble man in his fifties, is an especially gifted meditation leader. His ability to use the daily sessions to give us direct experience of the material we cover in classes is awe-inspiring.

Though it shifts somewhat with people's varied schedules, our class consists of about forty members. It is an ideal number and, as it turns out, an ideal group, each student gifted in a particular way that contributes to the richness of the whole. Though our backgrounds differ, a strong sense of camaraderie develops among us. Fundamental to this cohesion is our love of Vedanta, our devotion to Swami Dayananda and our continuing association with the ashram in some way.

After the frustration of seventeen years of Vedanta-two-weeks-at-a-time, I am now free to immerse myself in it, a luxury I have dreamt of, but of which I have no specific expectation. The *Prasnopanisad*, from the *Atharva Veda*, is a set of six thorough questions posed by six qualified students to their revered guru, Pippalada. As they progress, the topics deepen in abstraction and profundity, addressing the source of life; the nature of heavenly beings; the life force, or *Prana*; the three states of waking, dreaming, and deep sleep; meditation on *Om*; and, finally, consciousness in man, called *Brahman* or *Moksah*.

Sage Pippalada's answers lead his students to the ultimate knowledge of Unity Consciousness. Sankaracharya, always a thorough companion to any text, uses the

Socratic method of asking and answering the most vexing questions that might arise from the text to provoke thought in others, to uncover potentially hidden objections, and so more rigorously find and fix the truth. There are beautiful metaphors along the way, such as comparing enlightenment to the merger of the raging Ganges and of the reverential Yamuna, as they court the loss of name and form, flowing joyfully toward the sea, which rises to meet them, just as enlightenment is said to engulf the sincere seeker at his journey's end. Swami TV taught the *Upanishad* extremely well.

The *Bhagavad Gita* or the "Song of God" is always dramatic and inspiring, no matter how many times one hears it. In the second chapter, Krishna, an incarnate deity, reveals the heart of Vedic teaching to his well-equipped student, Arjuna, as they are poised between two armies, waiting for the "battle of life" to begin. Krishna stresses the importance of dispassion or of rising above the pairs of opposites (desire and aversion), of using discrimination, and, thus, of moving from ignorance to enlightenment. The *Bhagavad Gita*—as do the Vedas—advocates freedom in this lifetime, *here* and *now*, without waiting for death and heaven as one's reward. It is powerful in the hands of an average teacher and is exponentially so when wielded by a great teacher like Swami TV. Especially as he sped up the *Prasna* and slowed down the *Gita* so their messages converged, we confronted the same challenging argument, in different dress, several times a day. I glory in being at the ashram and listening to the teaching at this leisurely pace, which leaves time for meditation after every class, so the teaching is immediately more clear and solidly embedded in my mind.

Then, four weeks into the program, and forty-five minutes into the 11:15 class, a Sanskrit word, *tajus* or brilliance, which I recognize in the Devanagari Script before it is translated, fires a lightning bolt into my head and shorts out my brain, and, suddenly, things clear up. Speechless and at rest, my mind is transformed. *Total* silence envelops my being. Uncontrollable tears pour down my cheeks. I try to hide them so no one will interrupt the ecstasy I feel.

This new Self experiences its body as an unwanted "puppet" which can't be shaken off as it fairly stumbles around the now empty lecture hall. Finally, the Self gathers it up and takes it on a long, solitary walk.

The day is gorgeous, and in tranquility the world is as fresh and clean, as new creation. Without mental chatter or verbal fragments, silence is sanctity. It is *being* in the presence of God. Thoughts come as insights, comprehended with no words to disturb the holy indwelling. One such thought is reminiscent of first wearing glasses at age ten and seeing that trees—no longer green smudges—had individual leaves that fluttered and showed two sides of different hue, with veins and shapes unique from leaf to leaf and tree to tree. Clear physical sight was astonishing then, and clear "spiritual sight" is more astonishing now, as the sun filters through the golden leaves of fall, some thinning and crinkling, some paling green, splashed with reds and yellows. A bird's song, rich and vibrant, sounds inside the Self.

There is a breeze and a quiet joy, and *tajas*, the Sanskrit word from class. There is silence between bird songs and a feeling of limitless energy, unbound.

This new Self is the true self, *vinasi*, indestructible. Now, mirrors of perception cleansed, *satyam* rules *mithya*, and consciousness is where the heart had seemed before; each moment, serene; each image, new.

Meditation or *being* is continuous. Mind and body—the universe itself—await permission to manifest in this pristine, gloriously silent and immensely peaceful space.

> "In me,
> In the space of awareness
> Rises the celestial city
> Called the world.
> Therefore, How am I not
> *Brahman*, who is all knower
> And the cause of all." (1)

Movement of the mind appears on a changeless background as the play or *lila* of the Source. The world *is* a passing show. Swami Dayananda says succinctly, "If it be *satyam* not *mithya* then it is: 1) self-evident, 2) self-existent, and 3) non-negatable. Is there such a thing? There is, for in *Being*, we are *That:* Consciousness, Awareness, the only truth that is.

> Being the witness
> Is a relative definition.
> It is not the truth of my nature,
> For I am the ocean of Awareness,
> Free from all waves. (2)

In the beginning was the word, and the word was with God, and the word was God…. Hereafter ye shall see heaven open, and the angels of God ascending and descending upon the….” (3) illusion of Jacob’s ladder. For Consciousness is all there is, and, so, “such stuff as (worlds and) dreams are made of….” (4)

POSTSCRIPT:

This Therapist Looks at Ultimate Mental Health

As I grow accustomed to the Illumined Self, I see I had a preeminent stumbling block on my way to understanding Vedanta. Perhaps this problem—or certainly one of many fears and emotional dilemmas along the path toward self-knowledge—is not uncommon and therefore might be useful to share, as Swami Dayananda's sharing of his Dark Night conundrum about Vedanta as a *pramana* has been invaluable to many of his devotees.

My problem was that, no matter how many times I heard it and no matter how much I thought I understood it, I failed to grasp an essential fact until I was hit over the head with its truth as I have just described. That fact is that "the mind is consciousness, but consciousness is *not* the mind." It is ironic to me now that this is the theme of that first pamphlet, *Action and Reaction*, which I received from my Indian friend so long ago, the one which lead me to Swami Dayananda; "The actor is the role, but the role is not the actor," he wrote. The mind/body/sense complex is insentient matter, made conscious by reflecting the consciousness that contains it, the psychosomatic apparatus is really *mithya*, a projection by consciousness and, so, could never be its source. That's why the ESP example hit me so hard at the MIT lecture. It forced me to see myself and others as *dependent* on the Source, its agents, with no independent agency of our own. It is also why I needed the lightning bolt to bring absolute silence to my mind, so that reality might finally turn itself right side up, for even after seventeen years of study, I had clearly continued to live it upside down—as an *idea* in my mind and not as a core feeling in my *heart*.

This is also why, the masters say, "Enlightenment is beyond the mind." It's no trick of words, nor is it a statement to complicate matters, but one to convey the central truth of enlightenment. It's why Meister Eckhart could say, "God is nearer to me than I am to myself, (and) He is just as near to wood and stone, but they do not know it." Just as if I were wood and stone, I never really knew it either, until I was pushed off that tall tower of mind into the free-fall zone of *Consciousness*. I am *not* the body/mind/sense complex; they are *me*, but *I* am not *them*. I am consciousness alone. This is a strange truth to us habituated as we are to the notion of an independent self in a separate body. Nonetheless this is *the* essential "truth."

The maturation toward enlightenment takes time, but Self-realization is sudden, and yet I am still not settled into that final goal. Who knows how long a time I must wait, for that harder-than-diamond *core* of truth to take hold completely in the depths of my heart? I don't know, but, because the scriptures promise it *will* happen *someday,* I am no more afraid. Finally, I believe Lord Krishna's promise and am at peace, awaiting the will of God in blessed silence...

END NOTES

Introduction: Piaget's Cognitive Stages as a Platform for Emotional Development
(1)   Theorists agree that in the first weeks of life an infant does not yet know inside from outside and is functionally, albeit normally, psychotic.

Chapter Five: Piaget's Science of Psychology
(1)   Piaget. (1974), pp. 17—19.
(2)   Piaget (1974), pp. x and xi.
(3)   Kohut, Heintz. (1971).
(4)   Piaget. (1974), p. 210.
(5)   Ibid pp. 268—271 and pp. 284—285.

Chapter Seven: Second-Plateau Case Examples Juxtaposed with the First
(1)   Blos, P. (1962), pp. 9, 34.
(2)   Blank and Blank. (1986), p. 116.
(3)   Elliot. (1943). "Burnt Norton," Canto II, line 16.

Chapter Eight: Seeking Knowledge
(1)   Tattvavidananda Saraswati. p.16.
(2)   The sadhus discourse is a composite of his teaching and that of other Indians from Ganeshpuri.
(3)   Yukteswar, S. p. iii.

Chapter Nine: "When the Student Is Ready, the Teacher Appears"
(1)   The Vedic culture is unquestionably ancient but scholars and anthropologists have not confirmed the true age of the Indus Valley Civilizations, which include the cities of Harrapa, Mohenjo-Daro, Lothal,

Mehrgarth, the present town of Mithankot (in the southern Punjab). Early settlers established their cities along the rivers: the Indus, the Saraswati, the Narmada, the Yamuna, and the Ganges. They grew and stored barley, raised sheep and goats, constructed homes and other buildings of sun-baked mud bricks. New discoveries continue to move the first dates back in time. Some sources place the beginning of this civilization at 3,300 BCE, and even at 10,000 BCE when the Tattiriya Brahmana (3.1.2) refers to Purva hadrapada nakstra's rising due east,which occurred at this time, and others to 8,500 BCE when Taittiriya Samhita (6.5.3) places Pleades asterism at winter solstice, suggesting the antiquity of this Veda (see citation, p. 227).

(2)   This is a composite of many of Swami Dayananda's lectures, including material from the first one I heard him give at MIT in June of 1987.

(3)   "Bramaji" is the creative aspect of the Hindu Godhead. (See Tatvavidananda Saraswati, p. 41)

(4)   *Bhagavad Gita*, Chapter Two, verses 23 and 24.

Chapter Ten: Western Mystics and Eastern Wise Men: Stages of Spiritual Growth

(1)   Underhill. (1974), p. 199.
(2)   Ibid. p. 232 and 234
(3)   Hillesum. (1985), p. 14 and 15.
(4)   Underhill. (1974), p.199 and 200.
(5)   Underhill. (1974), p. 200.
(6)   Hillesum. (1985), p. 44.
(7)   Underhill. (1974), p. 202 and 203.
(8)   Ibid. p. 204.
(9)   Thoreau, p. 82 .
(10)   Underhill. (1974), p. 218.
(11)   Ibid. p. 214.
(12)   Ibid. p. 212.
(13)   Underhill. (1974), p. 228.
(14)   Hopkins. (1953), p. 27.
(15)   Underhill. (1974), p. 257 and 258.
(16)   Hillesum. (1985), p. 66, 72, and 76.

(17) Underhill. (1974), p. 240.

(18) Ibid. p. 422.

(19) Ibid. p. 239.

(20) Ibid. p. 265.

(21) C.G. Jung. (1953–1979), CW 11, par.773 and 961.

(22) Ibid. par. 17.

(23) Jung, (1953–1979), CW 11, par. 774.

(24) Ibid. par. 817–818.

(25) Underhill. (1974), p. 389 and 390.

(26) Ibid. p. 389

(27) Ibid. p. 386

(28) Hillesum. (1985), p. 87 and 231.

(29) Underhill. (1974), p. 368 and 389.

(30) Hillesum. (1985), pp. 87 and 231.

(31) Hillesum. (1985), p. 91 and 142.

(32) Underhill. (1974), p. 404.

(33) Ibid. p. 405.

(34) Ibid.

(35) Ibid. p. 406.

(36) Ibid. p. 410 and 411.

(37) Ibid. p. 412.

(38) Personal communication from Swami Dayananda, December 1990.

(39) Tolle. (1997), p.1.

(40) Ibid. p. 2.

(41) Ibid. p. 3.

(42) Whitfield. p. 191.

(43) Underhill. (1974), p. 102.

(44) Ibid. p. 412.

(45) Hillesum. (1985), p. 255.

Chapter Eleven: An End to Beginningless Ignorance

(1) Laksmidhara, p.13.

(2) Ibid., p. 53.

(3) Holy Bible, John c.I: v.1–5.

(4) Shakespeare. *The Tempest*, Act 4, Scene 1.

SOURCES

Amipa, Shereb Gyaltsen. *The Opening of the Lotus: Developing Clarity and Kindness*. London: Wisdom Publications, 1987.

Augustine of Hippo, Saint. *The Confessions*. (trans by Henry Chadwick), Oxford University Press. Oxford, 1998 Cambridge, 1908.

Balsekar, Ramesh S. *Pointers From Nisargadatta Maharaj*, Durham, NC: Acorn Press, 1983.

———. *Seeking Enlightenment—Why?* Mumbai, India: Zen Publications, 2005.

Benson, H. and M. Klipper. *The Relaxation Response*. New York: Avon Books, 1976.

Blackburn, A. *Now Consciousness: Exploring the World Beyond Thought*. Ojai, California: Idyllwild Books, 1983.

Black Elk. *Black Elk Speaks: Being the Life Story of a Holy Man of the Oglala Sioux*. Lincoln, NE: University of Nebraska Press, 1988.

Blake, William. *The Letters of William Blake*. Edited by A.G.B. Russell. London: Oxford Press, 1906.

———. *Poems and Prose of William Blake*. Edited by Geoffrey Keynes. London: Oxford Press, 1927.

———. *The Complete Illuminated Books*. Introdction by David Bindman. New York: Thames and Hudson, 2000.

Blanck, Rubin and Gertrude. *Beyond Ego Psychology*. New York: Columbia University Press, 1986.

Blos, P. *On Adolescence: A Psychoanalytic Interpretation*. New York: The Free Press, 1962.

Borysenko, J. *Minding the Body, Mending the Mind*. Reading, MA: AddisonWesley Publishing Company, Inc., 1987.

Boehme, Jacob, *The Works of Jacob Boehm 1764–81*.Tr. by William Law (4 vols.). London: Red Wheel/Weiser, 2000.

Bucke, Richard Maurice. *Cosmic Consciousness*. Secaucus, New Jersey: The Citadel Press, 1977.

Campbell, J. *Masks of God* (4 vols.). New York: Penguin, 1968.

Casti, J. *Paradigms Lost: Tacking the Universal Mysteries of Modern Science*. New York: Avon Books, 1990.

Catherine of Genoa. *Life and Doctrine*. New York: Christian Publishing Company, 1907.

Course in Miracles. (3 vols.). Foundation for Inner Peace: Tiburon, CA. 1987.

Dalai Lama XIV. *Opening the Eye of New Awareness*. Trans. by Donald S. Lopez Jr. with Jeffrey Hopkins). London: Wisdom Publications, 1985.

Dayananda, Sri Saraswati. *The Teaching of the Bhagavad Gita*. New Delhi and Bombay: Vision Books, 1987.

———. CD recorded at AVG circa 2000.

Dobson, John. "A Sidewalk Astronomer." DVD by Jeffery Fox

Eckhart, Meister. *Schriften und Predigten*, ed. von Gustov Landauer. Leipsig: University of Notre Dame Press, 1985.

———. *Mystisch Schiften*, ed. von Gustov Landauer. Berlin: New York Paulist Press, 1985

Eliot, T.S. *The Four Quartets*. New York: Harcourt, Inc., 1943.

Fast, I. *Selving: A Relational Theory of Self Organization*. Mahwah, NJ: The Analytic Press, 1998.

Jacobs Jacobs Entertainment Inc: Harrison, N. Y.1967.

en.wikipedia.org/wiki/Indus Valley Civilization. 21 November 2010.

Francis of Assisi. *Early Documents*. Ed.by Armstrong, Hellman, and Short. New York: New City Press, 1999.

Goodman, M. *The Last Dalai Lama*. Boston: Shambala, 1986.

Gyatso, G. *Heart of Wisdom*. London: Tharpa Publications, 1986.

Gyatso, T. *Kindness, Clarity, and Insight*. Trans. by Jeffrey Hopkins. Ithaca, NY: Snow   Lion Publications, 1984.

Hesse, H. *Siddhartha*. Trans. by Hilda Rosner. New York: New

Directions, 1957.

Hicks, R. and N. Chogyam. *Great Ocean: An Authorized Biography of The Dalai Lama*. Longmead, Shaftsbury, Dorset, Great Briton: Element Books, Ltd., 1984.

Hillesum, E. *An Interrupted Life: The Diaries of Etty Hillesum 1941–43*. Ed. by J.G. Gaafiandt. New York: Washington Square Press, 1985.

Hopkins, G.M. *Poems and Prose*. London: Penguin Poets Series, 1953.

Hopkins, J. *Meditation On Emptiness*. London: Wisdom Publications, 1983.

Inhelder, B. and J. Piaget. *The Growth of Logical Thinking from Childhood to Adolescence*. Trans. by A. Parsons and S. Milgrarn. New York: Basic Books, 1958.

Jacopone da Todi. *The Lauds*. Trans. by Serge and Elizabeth Hughes. New York: Paulist Press, 1982.

John of the Cross. *The Ascent of Mount Carmel*. Trans. by David Lewis. Oxford: Clarendon Press, 1908. *The Dark Night of the Soul*. Trans. by David Lewis. Paulist Press Classics: Mahwah, N. J.,2007.

Julian of Norwich. *Revelations of Devine Love* (8th ed.). Edited by Grace Warrack. London, 1923.

Jundt, A. *The Friends of God*. The Catholic Encyclopedia, (Vol 6: article by Charles George Hermann). St. Joseph, Minnesota: College of St. Benedict and St. John's University, 1913.

Jung, C.G. *The Collected Works* (20 vols.). Ed. by H.Read, M. Fordham, G. Adler, W. Mcguire and trans. by R.F.C. Hull. Princeton: Princeton University Press, 1953–1975.

Karma, Lingpa. *The Tibetan Book of the Dead*. Trans. by Francesca Fremantle and Chogyam Trungpa. London: Shambala, 1975.

Kegan, R. *The Evolving Self*. Cambridge, MA: Harvard University Press, 1982.

Klein, J. *The Ease of Being*. Durham, NC: The Acorn Press, 1984.

Kohut, H. *The Analysis of the Self: A Systematic Approach to the Psychoanalytic Treatment of the Narcissistic Personality Disorder*. Madison, Connecticut: International Universities

Press, Inc., 1971.

Krishnamurti, J. *Krishnamurti to Himself, His Last Journal.* San Francisco: Harper and Row, 1980.

———. *The Flame of Attention.* San Francisco: Harper and Row, 1984 .

Kutz, I., J. Borysenko, and H. Benson. "Meditation and Psychotherapy: A Rationale for the Integration of Dynamic Psychotherapy, the Relaxation Response, and Mindfulness Meditation." *The American Journal of Psychiatry,* 142, 1–8 (1985).

Law, William. *The Liberal and Mystical Writings of William Law, 1686–1761.* London: Longmans, Green, and Co., 1908.

Lao Tsu. *Tao Te Ching.* Trans. by Feng and English. New York: Vintage Books, 1972.

Laksmidha, Charakur. *Advaita Makaranda:* Translation and commentary by Ann Berliner. Asia Publishing House: Bombay: Published with arrangement with Shri Gangadhareshwara Trust. Bombay, India: Asia Publishing House, 1990.

Levine, Stephen. *A Gradual Awakening.* Garden City, NY: Anchor Books, 1979.

Lucie, Christine. *Spiritual Journal of Lucie-Christine (1870–1908).* London: Kegan Paul, 1915.

Maeterlinck, Maurice, "Introduction" to Ruysbroeck's *The Adornment of the Spiritual Marriage.* trans by Maurice Maeterlinck. New York: E. P. Dutton and Co.,1916,

Mahler, M.S., F. Pine, and A. Bergman. *The Psychological Birth of the Human Infant.* New York: Basic Books, Inc., 1975.

Mahoney, W.K. *The Artful Universe: An Introduction to the Vedic Religious Imagination.* Albany, NY: State University of New York Press, 1998.

Maslow, Abraham. *Toward a Psychology of Being.* New York: The Viking Press, 1971.

———. *The Farther Reaches of Human Nature.* New York: Viking Press, 1971.

Mouni Sadhu. *Meditation: An Outline for Practical Study.* North Hollywood, CA: Wilshire Book Company, 1967.

Muktananda, S. *The Play of Consciousness.* San Francisco: Harper and Row, 1974.

———. *I Am That*. Ganeshpuri, India: Syddha Foundation, 1978.

Nisargadatta Maharaj, S. *I Am That*. (Marice Frydman, Trans.). Durham, NC: Acorn Press, 1982.

———. *Prior to Consciousness: Talks with Sri Nisargadatta Maharaj*. Ed. by Jean Dunn. Durham, NC: The Acorn Press, 1985.

———. *The Nectar of the Lord's Feet*. Ed. by Robert Powell. Great Britain: Element Books, 1987.

Persig, R. *Zen and the Art of Motorcycle Maintenance*. New York: Morrow Quill Paperbacks, 1972.

Piaget, J. *The Child's Conception of the World*. London: Rutledge and Kegan Paul, Ltd., 1929.

———. *Play, Dreams and Imitation in Childhood*. New York: WW Norton & Company, Inc., 1962.

———. *Logic and Psychology*. Manchester, England: Manchester University Press, 1953.

———. *The Origins of Intelligence in Children*. New York: International Universities Press, Inc., 1974.

———. *The Grasp of Consciousness: Action and Concept in the Young Child*. Trans. by Susan Wedgwood. Cambridge, MA: Harvard University Press, 1976.

Plato. *Phaedo*. Trans. and ed. by David Gallop. Oxford, NY: Oxford University Press, 1993.

Powell, R. *The Blissful Life*. Durham, NC: The Acorn Press, 1984.

Ramakrishna, S. *The Gospel of Sri Ramakrishna*. Trans. by Swami Nikhilananda Myapore, Madras, India: Sri Ramakrishna Math, 1981.

Ram Dass. *The Only Dance There Is*. Garden City, NY: Anchor Books, 1974.

———. *Grist for the Mill*. New York: Bantam Books, 1977.

Ramana Maharshi. *The Spiritual Teaching of Ramana Maharshi*. Boston: Shambala, 1988.

———. *Talks with Sri Ramana Maharshi*. Tiruvannamalai, India: Venkataraman Press, Sri Ramanashraman, 1984.

Recejac, E. *Essay on the Bases of the Mystic Knowledge*. Trans. by Sara Carr. Scribner, 1899.

Ruysbroeck, John of. *Adornment of the Spiritual Marriage*. Trans. by

Wynschend J. M. Dent and Sons, Ltd : London, 1916.

Shakespeare, William. *The Tempest*. Published by Digireads.com Publishing: Stillwell, KS. 2005.

Shore, Allan N. *Affect Regulation and the Origin of the Self*. Hilldale, New Jersey: Lawrence Erlbaum Associates, 1994.

Sinetar, M. *Ordinary People as Monks and Mystics*. New York: The Paulist Press, 1986.

Spitz, R.A. *The First Year of Life: A Psychoanalytic Study of Normal and Deviant Development of Object Relations*. New York: International Universities Press, 1965.

Stevenson, R.L. *The Strange Case of Dr. Jekyll and Mr. Hyde*. Delaware: Prestwick House, 2005.

Subramanum, K. *Mahabharata*. Bombay: Bharatiya Vidya Bhavan, 1985.

Suso, Heinrich. *Leban und Schriften*. Trans by F. Tobin. New York: Paulist Press, 1989.

Tattvavidananda, Swami. *Inner Growth through Devotion*. India: Hyderabad, A.P., 2007. Teresa of Avila. *Interior Castle*. New York: Doubleday, 1989.

———. *The Way of Perfection*. Trans. by the Benedictines of Stabrook Abbey. Orleans, MA: Paraclete Press, 2009.

Thompson, A. "An Object-relational Theory of Affect Maturity: Applications to the Thematic Apperception Test." In M. Kissen (Ed.), *Exploring Object Phenomena Through Psychological Tests*. New York: International Universities Press, 1982.

Threau, Henry David. *Walden*. New York: Random House, Inc., 1965.

Tolle, Eckhart. *The Power of Now: A Guide to Spiritual Enlightenment. Vancouver, Canada:* Namaste Publishing Inc., 1997.

Tomkins, S. "Affect Theory." In P. Ekman (Ed.), *Approaches to Emotion*. Hillsdale, NJ: Guilford Press, 1984.

Underhill, E. *Mysticism: A Study in the Nature and Development of Man's Spiritual Consciousness*. New York: Penguin Books. 1974.

———. *Mystics of the Church*. Harrisburg, PA: Morehouse Publishing, 1975.

————. *Jacopone da Todi: Poet and Mystic: A spiritual Biography.* London and Toronto: J.M. Dent and Sons, 1919.

Unger, R.M. "A Program for Late TwentiethCentury Psychiatry." *American Journal of Psychiatry,* 139:2, pp. 155–164 (1982).

Whitfield, C. *The Jungian Myth and Advaita Vedanta.* Dissertation presented to faculty of the Graduate Theological Union at Berkeley, California. November 1992.

Yogananda, P. *Autobiography of a Yogi.* Los Angeles: SelfRealization Fellowship, 1979.

Yukteswar, S. *The Holy Science.* Los Angeles: SelfRealization Fellowship, 1979.

www.answerbag.com/q_view/524424. December 27th, 2007.

ABOUT THE AUTHOR

The author practiced psychotherapy for forty-five years. She began working as an untrained social worker in the welfare system, then took a two-year master's degree from Simmons College in Boston. She worked in medical hospitals, in mental hospitals, in child guidance clinics and in private practice. She married and raised a daughter.

She was trained both in dynamic and in developmental psychology. Her keen interest in growth and development lead her to immersion in Eastern spirituality, as the culmination of psychic evolution. She has successfully consolidated Western psychology and Eastern enlightenment (or Western sanctity), and she describes these final steps to Ultimate mental health in Part III of this book. She is now retired and lives on the South Coast of Massachusetts.

The author still enjoys the longer courses at AVP and also enjoys discovering new approaches to seeking enlightenment. Noteworthy among these is Bob Adamson from Australia, who received his knowledge from Nisargadatta

Maharaj in the 70s and has been teaching at his home ever since. He has been instrumental in the enlightenment of many people in the United States, with a cluster around San Jose, CA. He and those he has helped to find their "Natural State" (from the meaning of Nisargadatta as "nature giver") can be contacted through their website "The Urban Guru Café." Another very exciting source of spiritually interested and enlightened men and women can be accessed by internet through their interviews at Iain and Renate McNay's www.conscious.tv. This TV station was begun in 2007 in Britain and has by now hundreds of interesting interviews available for viewing.